Using Charts To Improve Profits

By Ely Francis

SUNVILLAGE
publications

www.sunvillagepublications.com

Using Charts To Improve Profits
By Ely Francis

Copyright © 2011

SUNVILLAGE
publications

Cover design by www.WebCopyAlchemy.com

Every man who knows how to read has it in his power to magnify himself, to multiply the ways in which he exists, to make his life full, significant and interesting. —
ALDOUS HUXLEY

INTRODUCTION

Charts are living proof that "a picture is worth a thousand words." Charts provide management with an easily understood review of a company's past, present and projected future. This book explains how charts can be used most effectively, and how profits can be improved through a well-thought-out chart program.

Many executives have difficulty in analyzing financial statements; they often have too little time to study interpretive reports. The solution to this major management problem of communication is a group of charts for total company, each division and the important product lines. These charts should review sales, costs, profits, percent to sales, return on investment, inventories and receivables. The annual periods covered will extend back five years and forward five years. The more current review will include monthly, quarterly and year-to-date information for last year, this year and next year.

This book explains how the proper comparisons of operating results in chart form can alert management to unfavorable sales, cost, profit, inventory and receivable trends. It also explains how charts can effectively highlight the consequences of alternate courses of action. A series of charts and schedules, beginning with Chapter 5, illustrates how a company can utilize a simple chart program for controlling its sales and cost trends, and maximizing its profits. The charts not only depict a coordinated set of figures, but also serve to demonstrate different types of chart presentations. It must be recognized that space does not permit every type of chart variation; those used in this book are basic, easy to use, and are recommended for management action. It was also considered impractical to portray how each month, each quarter and each year would appear in each type of chart. These refinements would follow a normal course in constructing a coordinated set of charts.

It is suggested that any chart program adopt three basic standards:

1. Have supporting statistical schedules available when reviewing the charts.
2. Have interpretive comments ready which explain why changes have occurred.
3. Present the type of chart which most easily depicts the individual situation.

Charts are a very important management tool and this book explains how best to use them.

ELY FRANCIS

CONTENTS

LIST OF CHARTS

Using the Pie Chart

Following the Sales Trend

Using Charts to Control Costs

Using Charts to Evaluate Profits

USING CHARTS
TO IMPROVE
PROFITS

WHAT CHARTS CAN ACCOMPLISH

Charts are a forceful means of presenting vital information to corporate management. They are industry's proof of the expression "A picture is worth a thousand words."

This book is designed to give management an appreciation of what charts can do through a clearer understanding of the company, its products and its future.

Charts tell a story which pages of statistics and interpretive comment cannot match. Trends of past performance can be related to forecasts of future plans. Preliminary estimates can be plotted, revised and put in final form on a chart in a relatively short period of time. The preparation of comparable pages of statistical summary and subsidiary schedules, in a formalized style, could conceivably require many additional hours by a large number of people.

Charts should be used more extensively by executives, especially those individuals who have difficulty struggling through statistical reports or who have insufficient time to read all the interpretive comments flowing across their desks each day.

Every facet of a company's operation can be charted, either in summary form, or in great detail, by operating unit, or by individual cost and expense categories. Charts can be easily updated using several different techniques. It is suggested that each month's financial data be entered on the charts at the time the accounting reports are issued.

It is recommended that a company begin its charting program on a modest and realistic basis. It is usually best to begin with total sales, profits, assets, profit ratio to sales, asset turnover and return on assets. Any attempt to launch a full-scale program, which includes each division and its product lines and all the pertinent data relating to them, is likely to result in confusion, undue delays, misinterpretation and a breakdown of sensible planning. These additional charts should be included after the total company charts have been carefully prepared, reviewed by management and selected as a basis for periodic business review meetings.

The charts should be readily accessible to the top corporate management at all times. The charts relating to individual divisions should be available to the divisional management. However, it is essential, when a discussion of charts is scheduled, that a member of the financial department be present to properly interpret the data under discussion. Too often scales are misread, headings are overlooked, technical information is misinterpreted and conclusions are erroneously drawn. This points up the necessity for having top management participate in the final decision regarding the basic chart style to be used. It is of no value to receive management support for a chart program and then to present all company data on charts which cannot be understood. At the same time the management should indicate a preference for line charts versus bar charts, or a sensible blending of both. This type of direction from the top can help both the executive and those charged with the responsibility for presenting the material. At the inception of a chart program the corporate controller should have alternate charts prepared and review them with the executive management, explaining what can be expected from the charts and what information is adaptable to charts.

Any company embarking on a chart program would do well to follow a fundamental principle of chart preparation and availability. Before any charts are shown to a member of the operating or top executive management, they should be thoroughly reviewed by the top financial officer of the company, so that he is fully prepared to answer any questions. This is made easier if the charts are kept in a room especially designed for the review of charts. It can then be agreed that no charts will be displayed prior to their receiving approval from a designated financial officer of the company. This basic procedure will do much to insure the success of a chart program. Each chart should be accompanied by interpretive comments. This is illustrated by the comments which follow each statistical schedule in this book.

The most effective charts are the simple ones. Any chart which attempts to compress too much diversified information onto one graph is doomed to failure. It is also liable to create the impression that charts cannot assist the management in easily understanding the business. Just as charts need not be complex, neither must they be fancy or elaborate. While a chart prepared by a professional, with a background in mechanical drawing or commercial art, will look better than one drawn by an amateur, the message, if properly presented, will be just as factual and easy to understand in either instance.

2

THE INITIAL STEPS

It is necessary to employ a systematic, step-by-step approach to the adoption of a company-wide chart program. There are a number of practical considerations. First, where should the program begin.

Total Company Approach

It is logical to have the first charts prepared for the use of the executive management. A chartist can be hired and a chart room set aside. Someone, preferably a member of the financial organization, should be officially designated in charge of the chart preparation, the chart room, the statistical information required, and the explanatory data which accompanies each chart. A person with accounting or statistical training should prepare the data to be plotted on the charts.

Following the lead of the corporate office, the divisions and subsidiaries can prepare chart rooms and pattern their chart presentations after the executive program. The divisional and subsidiary charts should contain most of the top level information which appears in the executive office chart room; this will be supplemented by a number of detail charts which depict the many control items the operating management uses to direct day-to-day activities. For example, the top corporate management is mainly interested in sales, profits, assets, inventories, receivables, profit per cent to sales and per cent return on assets. In addition to these, the operating managers must get into cost and expense control item by item, production scheduling by models, product movement through the distributor-dealer pipeline, inventory buildups prior to new model introduction dates, the cost and effect of special promotions, and similar, more fragmentary problems. All of these activities require final decisions after considering alternate courses of action.

A coordinated chart program can be most effective at the time discussion centers on the results of alternate courses of action. The operating executive can be given a voluminous report or a series of statistical schedules detailing all the pros and cons. A superior approach would be a simple set of charts, prepared to illustrate what will happen, for instance, to profits if the company increases expenses to support a higher sales volume and then the business fails to materialize. These alternates are demonstrated in chart form in later chapters of this book.

If the reader is going to adopt a top company chart program before going to the divisional and product line level, it is suggested that the following program be considered. Begin with total company statistics going back as far as possible or as far as desired. Plot sales, profits, receivables, inventories, assets, fixed assets, net worth, equity and debt relationships, the essential ratios such as profit per cent to sales, per cent return on assets, asset turnover, current asset ratio and so on. In addition, some companies may have important single items which contribute materially to profit performance, such as engineering and development, raw material purchases, direct labor or traveling expenses. These should also be included in the basic series of charts, in order that all levels of management can review them and become acquainted with the important elements affecting company operations.

These charts should contain space for future years, to minimize the frequency of repeating the entire series. It is recommended that these historical charts not be used to plot short term forecasts or five-year plans. The historical charts should reflect only long term trends, and generally this is confined to total company operations. In some cases these charts are segmented by the years the company was served by different presidents, to compare sales and profit performance during each period.

Once the total company historical charts are completed, it is advisable to consider a series which will look to the future. Again focusing attention on the total company, it is suggested that space be provided for five years of history and a minimum of five years ahead. Actually, much time, effort and expense will be saved if this set of charts provides for 10 years into the future, even though forecasts extend out only five years at a time. The charts can be prepared using tape and as estimates change, the tape can be shifted to a new position without damaging the basic chart.

When these total company charts are completed, showing five years of history and future plans, it becomes quite obvious that developing trends are easily discernible; either the company is going up, is sliding downward, or has reached a plateau. Naturally, the management wishes to grow and become more profitable. The question arises, what should be the objective, what is a realistic goal. Oftentimes the answer lies in an examination of competitor performance. A natural complement to a total company chart presentation is the plotting of competitor data on the same chart. While it is not always possible to find companies with the exact product lineup as yours, each firm does compete directly with a number of other leaders in the same industry. A rather elementary, but important, rule should be adopted by the person in charge of the chart program. The selected competitor or competitors should have a better performance than your company, either from the standpoint of dollars of profit, per cent profit to sales or return on assets. This provides your management with a realistic goal to catch and pass a superior firm. Nothing is gained by comparing yourself with an inferior competitor. An example of how conditions can change and a company can be overtaken is illustrated by Chart 39 in Chapter 9. These competitor type charts should follow the usual format of five years backward and five years forward. They need not be elaborate, but should stress the most important basic operating criteria of sales, profits, assets, profit per cent to sales and return on assets.

It is appropriate, in the context of chart program costs, to make an important observation at this time. A chart program can be kept simple and inexpensive only if the management will take the time to decide, before its inception, on the chart format and objectives. If this is given little or no consideration at the outset, or a decision is made to go into a chart program to see what will develop, the operation will most likely fail. A chart program, like any other company-wide venture, must be given thorough consideration at the executive level, a responsible person must be in charge, a systematic approach must be adopted, the charts must be kept up to date and they must be used as a management tool. Charts are not a magic cure-all. Their effectiveness is directly proportionate to the effort going into them and the use made of them.

Divisional Approach

If a divisional chart program is developed initially a somewhat different approach is in order. Historical data probably need not extend back more than five years. In some cases it may be necessary to re-classify historical data to coincide with current product alignments. The emphasis should be placed on current and forecast information. Total divisional performance should include sales, profits, assets, receivables, inventories, profit per cent to sales, per cent return on assets, fixed assets, and major items peculiar to the division such as raw materials, direct labor, engineering, tooling, advertising, etc.

Once the basic divisional data is charted, the major effort should be devoted to product line objectives. This should be the main concern of the operating management, to make certain that the individual segments add to a satisfactory divisional total. Product line charts can add to an impressive total or they can be few in number. It is useless to *begin* on a grand scale. First, time, space and personnel will not permit the initial construction of many charts. Secondly, the management must be educated to using and understanding charts. Also, the people supplying the statistical data and those using it must pass through an adjustment period, to clarify what is needed, when, how it will be used and where it emanates. The first attempt at charting product line information will probably be restricted to sales, profits and the profit ratio to sales, unless the monthly accounting statements provide detailed breakdowns of all costs and expenses. The author feels this book is not the place to get into the controversy over expense allocations to product lines, the segregation of cash, inventories and receivables to product categories, etc. Assuming that product line detail is available, the author recommends that a series of charts be developed which will eventually provide the management with complete operating information. This will cover at least sales, profits, assets, cash, receivables, inventories, profit per cent to sales, and return on assets. Depending upon the individual operating needs, additional charts should include data on material purchases, direct labor, factory overhead, engineering, tooling, warranty, labelling and packaging, warehousing, freight, selling, advertising and promotion, credit and collection, bad debts and other items which may be more important to one company than another.

To summarize the recommended divisional chart program, there are three levels of charts to consider:

1. The total divisional series which is used at the executive cor porate level.
2. The total divisional charts showing more detailed information.
3. The product line information, gradually developed from the sales and profit concept to a detailed examination of essential operating elements.

Statistical Schedules

These should be developed along with the basic chart planning. The best place to begin is the weekly, monthly and annual accounting reports. An examination of these will indicate the extent of sales, profit and other data available for the total company, each division and subsidiary, and by individual product line. The person in charge of the chart program should contact the controller or director of accounting to thoroughly explore what is available compared with the chart requirements. For example, the data going back over the corporation's history may be incomplete or non-existent beyond five years. It may be desirable to assign an accountant to compile a complete financial history of the company. These have many important references apart from charting trend lines; this data can be used in litigation, answering stockholder inquiries, in addresses by major corporate executives and as comparisons with the development of competitors.

Although the accounting department will be the main source of operating statistics, the sales department oftentimes has detailed tabulations affecting product movement, distributor sales, industry averages, salesmen's performance, market penetration, the effectiveness of one district versus another and other related information.

Likewise, the market research department will have important data on economic factors such as gross national product, the industrial production index, the labor market, unemployment, labor rates, construction, industrial and consumer spending, consumer credit, mortgage financing, durable versus non-durable versus service purchases and all the other indices which are useful to both specific industries and the individual companies in them. This type of information should be analyzed by the corporate economist or someone in the controller's department to determine the relationship between a definite index and the company's sales and profit curve. Once this background material is developed, charts can be prepared which forcefully illustrate direct relationships between economic factors and the company's operating results.

Data affecting factory sales and costs should be secured from the plant accounting personnel and used to chart the most important items. Again, this type of data will necessitate a number of conferences to determine what is available, who will supply it, when it will be prepared and most important of all, how it will be used. It is just as important to obtain the understanding and cooperation of the lower management group in inaugurating a chart program as it is to sell it to the top corporate executives. Therefore, once the source of the statistics is determined, the person responsible for the chart program must meet with the various management echelons to secure their understanding of the purpose and advantages of a chart program. The beginning of a chart program in many ways resembles the installation of a budgetary control system; many people mistrust and oppose it until they are convinced of its benefits. The task of selling charts to management is every bit as important as the actual chart presentation.

Once the statistical sources are determined and timing schedules are agreed upon, the actual use of the figures can begin. It is suggested that simplified forms be prepared for the use of the chartist. These should contain only the headings he should use and not a lot of other superfluous and explanatory data. This can be attached to the schedules given the chartist, so that necessary references are not lost, but his material should not be cluttered. In addition to the proper headings, the chartist's schedule should contain the periods to be shown, the scale to be used, the figures to be plotted, the kind of data such as sales, profits, etc., whether the statistics represent dollars, units, pounds, etc., and the legend applicable to each piece of information. All of these rudiments should be arranged the same way each time, to avoid needless delay and misinterpretation. It must be remembered that most chartists have a creative flair, but they are usually not accountants or statisticians. It is generally well to request suggestions from the chartist regarding the proper layout, size of headings, scale spacings and other technical features. However, care should be exercised to make certain that a standard format persists throughout all the chart presentations, in order that the management may concentrate on interpreting the data being plotted and not be distracted by a mere lack of uniformity.

Updating the Charts

The periodic updating of charts is not only essential, but must be carefully scheduled. Monthly charts should be updated as soon as possible after the release of the official financial statements. As a practical matter, the chart updating should occur while the financial statements are being typed. This simultaneous release of the charts and the statements will permit the management to observe the more important trends on the charts at the same time they have the supporting statistical detail which is not charted. Weekly chart information must be plotted the same day it is received for maximum effectiveness. The weekly charts are best prepared in 8½" by 11" size to facilitate fast reproduction by photostat, multilith, fax copying or some other process. This permits immediate distribution and allows the management to review the data the day after it has been compiled. Proper scheduling of the chartist's time for updating is essential for one other reason. As the chart program receives its proper recognition, there will be increasing demands from many departments for special presentations. In order to avoid a complete disruption of the normal chart program, the following policy should be adopted. *Only* the person responsible for the chart program should decide when special requests can be accommodated. If this rule is not adopted, or if it is violated by anyone from the company president down, the entire program will degenerate into chaos; the alternative is a slippage in updating important chart information affecting the operation of the business. Since this is the primary responsibility of any good chart program, it must be accorded absolute priority.

Interpretive Comments

Charts tell a dramatic story and tell it quickly and concisely. However, charts perform no miracles, and like any other tool, require assistance. In addition, most of today's business is complicated and there are many factors underlying any statistical portrayal. A simple example of this lies in the comparison of sales and profits for this year and last year. One or the other may appear completely out of line. However, two frequent answers involve the mix of product or an unusually large order from one customer in one period versus a series of small orders in a similar comparative period.

For these and a number of other reasons, each chart should be accompanied by an explanation of the important influencing factors. A series of hypothetical statements have been used in this book following each statistical schedule to illustrate the technique. The actual explanation for any chart must, of course, be governed by the circumstances as they exist. It is necessary, though, to plan for this review as the chart program is being considered, as charts are developed and at the time they are being updated.

The responsibility for these explanations should rest with the individual in charge of the chart program. The logic of this is governed by the fact that he determines what charts are necessary, he arranges for the inflow of the statistical data, he sells the chart program to the management and finally, he schedules the preparation, updating and distribution of the charts. It is possible, however, to have the responsibility rest with the financial analyst who assists in the preparation of the accounting reports. In other cases, a specialist in the sales or market research department or in the plant may prepare the comments for the charts which affect these specialized areas. The final determination on this selection will rest with the management, and depend upon the company's organizational structure. However, it is so important that it must be considered in tandem with the charts themselves and the statistical data they reflect.

Type of Chart

This book illustrates varying formats for line charts, bar charts and pie charts. There are, of course, countless variations. However, nothing is gained by parading before the reader an endless succession of pictures when a few basic presentations will do the job properly and eliminate confusion and indecision.

It is the author's contention that the type of chart for any particular organization depends entirely upon the preferences of those using them, just as the use of charts versus statistical schedules is a matter of individual taste. If the message cannot be understood using a line chart, a bar chart or a pie chart, then quite possibly charts are not the proper medium.

Chapter 6 shows the effect to be obtained by applying line and bar charts to the same type of material. The pie chart has a much more restricted use and as a result has fewer illustrations. The bar and line charts predominate and are used interchangeably for purposes of demonstration. The author feels that the subject matter and the periods of time being covered should govern whether to employ a line or bar chart. There is no formula for determining which to use. When a question arises with regard to which is best, prepare the same data on each type of chart, present it to the person who will use the chart and then make a determination. In a short time, the person in charge of the chart program will have no difficulty with a selection. A series of line and bar charts, plus some examples of pie charts, are contained in Chapter 6.

3

TEN REQUIREMENTS FOR GOOD CHARTS

Definite rules must be established and adhered to if a chart program is going to be effective in contributing to greater profits through better understanding of the business.

A series of charts should not be attempted until all levels of management involved agree in principle on the major areas to be covered by the charts, the type of charts to be drawn and the purpose and use of the charts. To be most effective charts should follow these principles :

1. Use lines and bars where each is most meaningful. Don't become arbitrary and exclude one or the other.
2. Specific colors should designate like information.
3. Make it simple to construct and easy to understand.
4. Make it easy to update and revise the information.
5. Avoid overloading of data or too many subjects on one chart.
6. Use easily interpreted scales.
7. Use scales that match the requirements of the maximum amount of data and not necessarily extend to the ultimate range of the data.
8. Have uniform size chart paper.
9. Have all headings in the same place and commensurate in size with the over-all dimensions of the chart.
10. Make charts neat in appearance, with evenly spaced numbers and letters. The headings, scales, and time periods should be

15

centered, or balanced, for maximum attractiveness and reading ease.

1. *Use Lines or Bars Where Each Is Most Meaningful. Don't Exclude One or the Other.*

Lines or bars are usually the easiest to understand. Each serves a definite need. For example, bars generally are better suited when comparing one year's profit with another, or comparing another company's results with your own. Line charts can be very useful to indicate the trend of sales or profits over a period of time. Lines are oftentimes best employed when the sales or profits of several companies or divisions of the same company appear on one chart. There are no hard and fast rules governing when to use bars and when to use lines. It is usually a matter of judgment on the part of the chart maker or a matter of preference expressed by the chart user. It is important, however, not to become arbitrary and exclude the use of one or the other. Specific examples of this appear in Chapter 6 where an entire series of weekly, monthly, quarterly, annual and combined annual and quarterly sales charts are reproduced in both line and bar chart form.

2. *Specific Colors Should Designate Like Information.*

The people who use the charts will adapt to them more easily if they become accustomed to seeing the same information depicted in the same color on all charts. For example, black for sales, green for profits, red for losses, and varying shades of orange and yellow for ratios such as profit per cent to sales, return on assets, etc. As a practical illustration the following colors and legends can be used for pertinent operating information:

COLORS AND LEGENDS FOR CHARTS

Item	Color	Legend
Sales	Black	
Profits	Green	
Losses	Red	
Assets	Blue	
Profit % to Sales	Orange	
Return on Assets	Yellow	
Receivables	Brown	
Inventories	Purple	
Fixed Assets	Gold	
Costs	Silver	
Expenses	Light Blue	
Bad Debts	Light Green	

These illustrations do not exhaust the possibilities of colors or legends, but will serve to get the chart people started and will remove one additional detail for them to consider at the outset of a new and perhaps unfamiliar program.

The use of legends is almost mandatory when the charts are going to be reproduced, because many colors will not register upon duplication and when they do appear at all, it is in varying shades of black and gray.

The legends shown here come in black, blue, green and red and in the following sizes, ¼, 8, 2z and Q.

3. *Make It Simple to Construct and Easy to Understand.*

The use of lines or bars are suggested for easy preparation and understanding. If bars are used it is generally best to put the total at the end or top of each bar. If lines are used, the figures being plotted should be indicated about every 3 years. If more than one line appears on a chart it should be identified by a distinctive color, or legend or the name of the item being represented should be printed on the chart, with an arrow pointing to the line. Another technique is to place the name of the product line, expense item, etc. in the space between the lines, to indicate the area it represents on the chart. Any of these techniques makes each line distinctive and avoids confusion, particularly if several lines are close together or if they intersect. These suggestions are depicted on the accompanying Line Chart 1 and Bar Chart 2.

4. *Make It Easy to Update and Revise the Data.*

When forecasts of future operations or preliminary actual information is being plotted, the lines or bars should not be inked onto the chart. It is recommended that special colored chart tape be pasted onto the chart or onto a special cellophane chart cover or sleeve. The tape can be removed as revisions dictate. This tape is easy to apply and is neat in appearance and can be purchased in colors which match exactly the ink being used on other chart areas.

It is important that a temporary type sticker be attached to each chart indicating the date of the last revision. This is especially important when some charts are going to be updated monthly, others quarterly, etc. This sticker can appear in the lower right or left hand corner and not detract from the appearance of the chart, or interfere with the heading.

5. *Avoid Overloading of Data or Too Many Subjects on One Chart.*

It is far better to have two charts than to crowd too much information onto one. The person studying the chart can absorb only a limited quantity of statistics relating to one subject. This problem should not be compounded by introducing several subjects on the same chart. For instance, receivables and inventories should be kept on separate charts; sales and profits should not be combined; etc. An example of what can happen when too much information is assigned to one chart is illustrated by Chart 3. Although this chart deals with only one subject, sales, it is almost impossible to follow the company's factory and distributor sales on both a monthly and a year to date basis when comparing budget and actual results.

6. *Use Easily Interpreted Scales.*

The chart should provide a clear indication of whether the information is being expressed in units, dollars, pounds, and whether the quantities are in hundreds, thousands, millions, etc. In addition, the scale should have easily interpreted sections of 5's, 10's, 20's, etc. rather than odd breaks of 13's, 18's, etc. If the viewer cannot understand the scale it will be impossible for him to interpret the data. This elementary fact is frequently overlooked.

It is recommended that, where possible, only one scale appear on a chart and that this scale appear on both the left and the right margin. Dual scales are sometimes difficult to understand and may result in a misinterpretation of the data. The most frequently used dual scales appear on receivables and inventory charts. While some charts of the dual scale type cannot be avoided, this procedure is not recommended. Where weekly and monthly information appears with year to date figures, dual scales are necessary. However, those using the charts should be consulted before this procedure is adopted on a company wide basis.

7. *Scales Should Match the Requirements of the Maximum Amount of Data.*

Good judgment must be exercised by those using charts as well as those preparing them. A proper evaluation is impossible if the information being charted is improperly presented. For example, if profits for a product line have been fluctuating between $20,000 and $90,000 for 9 out of 10 years, the scale should range from zero to $100,000 even though profits in one year were $300,000. This one exceptional year can be indicated by the line running to the top of the chart, or the scale can be broken. Either solution is better than having a scale from zero to $300,000 with 9 years of information compressed into too small an area.

8. *Chart Taper Should Be Uniform in Size.*

Even though a chart program begins on a modest scale, consideration must be given to the problem of display and storage. This will be easier if the charts are uniform in size. Two very workable sizes are 30" by 40" and 20" by 30". The tendency to use exceptionally large charts carries with it a danger of crowding too much data onto the chart, making it hard to prepare, difficult to interpret, and impossible to store.

9. *Have All Headings in the Same Place and Commensurate in Size With the Over-all Dimensions of the Chart.*

The best acceptance of a chart depends to a considerable extent on maximum standardization. The headings should always be in the same place on every chart. The size of the headings as well as the size of other words and figures should be commensurate in size with the overall dimensions of the chart. Attention to these details give the chart a professional appearance and eliminates petty irritations which mitigate against an otherwise acceptable presentation. An example of a good and bad heading is shown for television receivers. Suggestions regarding the size of headings in relation to the dimensions of the chart appear under the caption, "Headings." Suggestions relating to scale sizes are contained on the schedule labeled "Scales."

10. *Neat Appearance.*

The people using a chart should insist that the headings, scales, time periods and other information be properly centered and neatly presented. There is no excuse for a poorly prepared chart any more than for its portraying inaccurate information. There are a number of publications available from chart supply firms which contain fundamental information on how to lay out and prepare basic charts. Once the outline of the chart is decided upon, care should be exercised to evenly space the letters and figures. A series of charts lose their appeal and effectiveness if they are not neat or carefully prepared. The over-all effect of the right way to prepare a chart is shown on Chart 4 and is compared with the total appearance when the same information is handled incorrectly, as on Chart 5.

PROPER ALIGNMENT OF HEADING

TELEVISION   RECEIVERS
• UNIT SALES •
LAST 3 YEARS

IMPROPER ALIGNMENT OF HEADING

UNIT   SALES OF TELEVISION RECEIVERS FOR THE LAST 3 YEARS

HEADINGS

ALL THE CHARTS IN THIS BOOK WERE DONE WITH THE AID OF MECHANICAL LETTERING GUIDES. THE HEIGHT OF LETTERS RANGES FROM O.IO (V!.!)) OF AN INCH TO 0.70 INCH. GUIDES ARE AVAILABLE FROM 0.05 INCH SIZE IN INCREASING STEPS TO THE LARGE SIZE OF 2.0 INCHES.

ORIGINALLY THE CHARTS IN THIS BOOK WERE 18"X24". WITH A 3 LEVEL HEADING, THE TOP LINE LETTERS WOULD BE 0.70" HIGH, THE MIDDLE LEVEL LETTERS 0.50" HIGH AND THE BOTTOM LEVEL 0.35" HIGH.

HOW TO DESIGN A PROPER HEADING:

MAINLINE CORPORATION
• BOWLING BALLS •
FACTORY UNIT SALES

BASED ON A STANDARD 3 LEVEL HEADING, LETTER HEIGHTS BY CHART SIZES ARE RECOMMENDED AS FOLLOWS:

CHART SIZE	TOP LINE	MIDDLE LINE	BOTTOM LINE
8½ X II in.	0.29 in.	0.24 in.	0.20 in.
II X 14	0.35	0.29	0.24
20 X 30	0.70	0.50	0.35
30 X 40	1.35	1.00	0.70

WHEN CHARTS USE TWO LEVEL HEADINGS, THE HEIGHT OF THE LETTERING FOR THE TOP AND BOTTOM LINES SHOULD BE THE SAME HEIGHT AS THE LETTERS USED IN THE TOP AND MIDDLE LINES OF A 3 LEVEL HEADING. THIS MAY VARY ACCORDING TO THE JUDGEMENT OF THE CHARTIST.

SCALES

HOW TO DESIGN A PROPER SCALE:

THE HEIGHT OF THE SCALE NUMBERS SHOULD BE COMPATIBLE WITH THE SIZE OF THE HEADINGS. THE FOLLOWING SCALE SIZES ARE RECOMMENDED, BUT MAY ALSO VARY ACCORDING TO THE JUDGEMENT OF THE CHARTIST.

RECOMMENDED HEIGHT OF SCALE NUMBERS:

CHART SIZES	NUMBER OF GRID LINES		
	5	10	15
82X II in.	0.14 in.	0.12 in.	0.10 in.
II X 14	0.175	0.14	0.12
18 X 24	0.24	0.20	0.175
20 X 30	0.35	0.29	0.24
30 X 40	0.50	0.425	0.35

EXHIBIT FOR LINE CHART 1
Actual Divisional Sales for 2 Years and a 10-Year Forecast

BOAT DIVISION

PRODUCT LINE SALES
($ In Millions)

	Motors	*Navigation*	*Hulls*	*Interiors*	*Total*
Last Year	10	10	30	5	55
This Year	15	12	35	10	72
Next Year	25	15	40	20	100
2 Years	35	30	45	30	140
3 Years	50	50	48	35	183
4 Years	60	65	50	40	215
5 Years	75	80	55	42	252
6 Years	85	95	60	45	285
7 Years	100	125	65	50	340
8 Years	115	150	75	55	395
9 Years	130	175	80	60	445
10 Years	145	200	95	65	505

Comments

Exhibit 1 and Line Chart 1 illustrate how long-term trends can be developed for a number of divisional operations and for the total company. There are several techniques for identifying each division. If the size of each segment permits, the name of the operating unit can be inserted as shown. If some or all of the pieces are small, the names can be listed on the chart border, or a colored legend can relate to the different areas.

This type of presentation is highly recommended because it permits the reviewer to readily evaluate trends, particularly over a long period of time. This is considered, by the author, as the best technique for depicting this type of information.

CHART 1

Boat Division
SALES

($ MILLIONS)

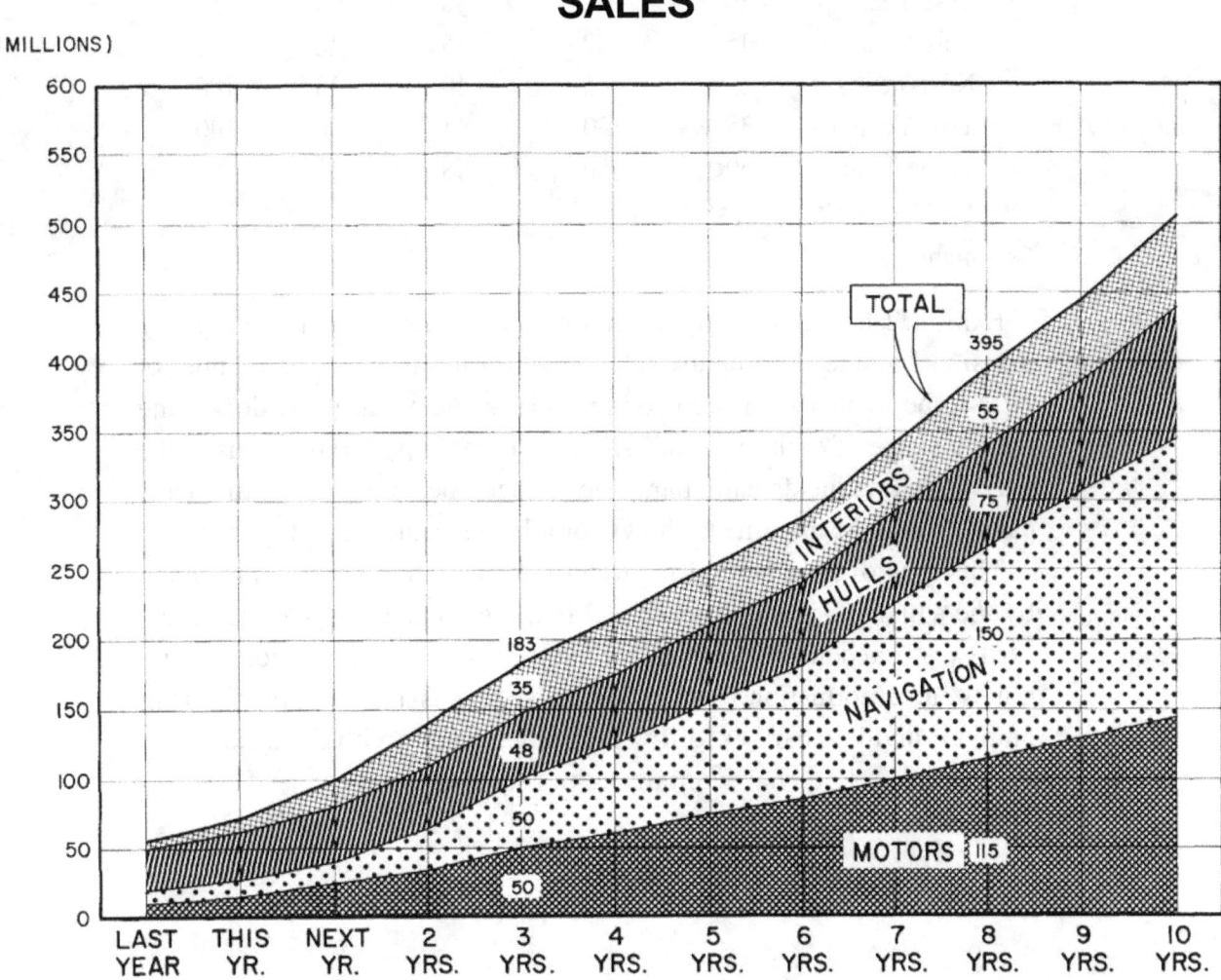

EXHIBIT FOR BAR CHART 2
Actual Divisional Sales for 2 Years and a 3-Year Forecast

BOAT DIVISION

PRODUCT LINE SALES
($ In Millions)

	Motors	Navigation	Hulls	Interiors	Total
Last Year	10	10	30	5	55
This Year	15	12	35	10	72
Next Year	25	15	40	20	100
Two Years	35	30	45	30	140
Three Years	50	50	48	35	183

Comments

Exhibit 2 and Bar Chart 2 demonstrate a technique for preparing divisional and total company sales trend information over a number of years. The methods for identifying each segment can vary, depending upon the size of each division's sales. While it is preferable to have the division name inside each bar, when space does not permit, the name can be along the margin, as shown, or a legend can be employed.

This type of presentation for trend information is *not* recommended by the author, for several reasons. First, the number of years is necessarily restricted unless the bars are made so thin they can accommodate almost no information. Secondly, the segments increase in differing amounts and it is hard to follow individual trends with the ease that is possible on a line chart containing the same data.

CHART 2

Boat Division
PRODUCT LINE SALES
($ MILLIONS)

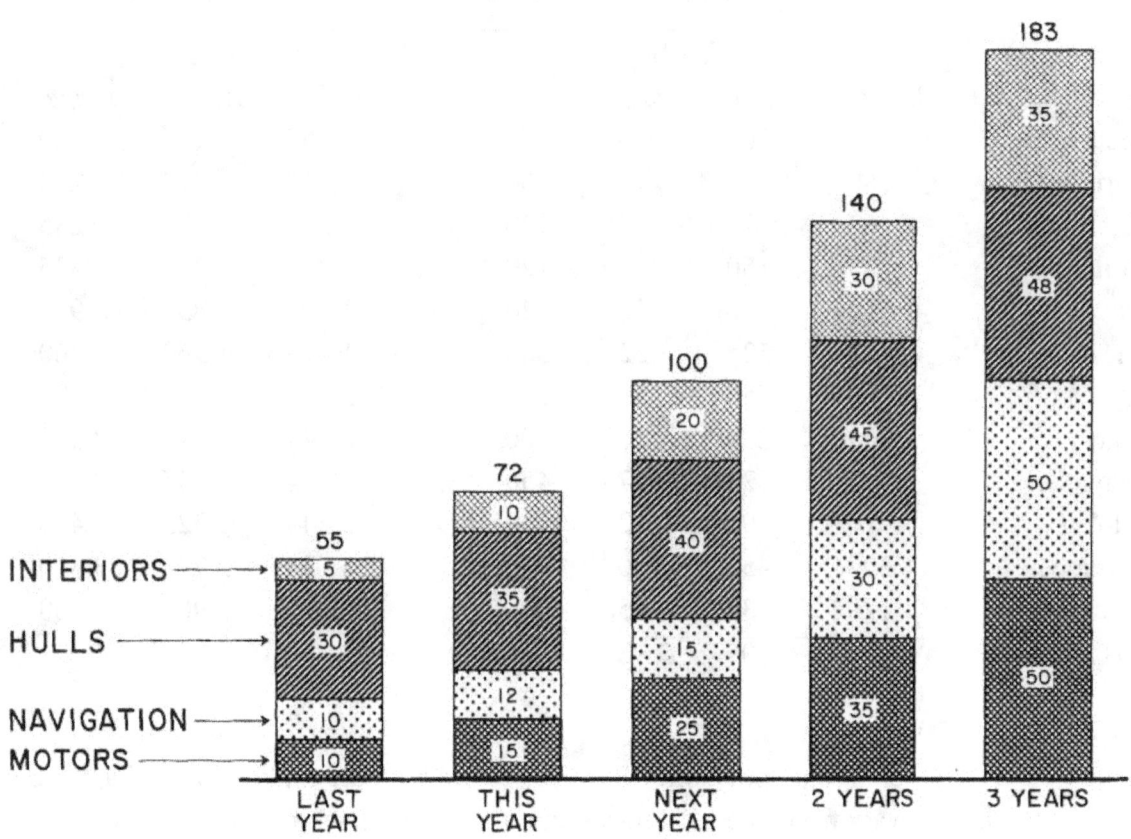

EXHIBIT FOR LINE CHART 3

Actual and Budgeted Monthly and Year to Date Factory and Distributor Unit Sales

BOAT DIVISION

UNIT BOAT SALES

THIS YEAR

	Monthly				Year to Date			
	Factory		Distributor		Factory		Distributor	
Month	*Budget*	*Actual*	*Budget*	*Actual*	*Budget*	*Actual*	*Budget*	*Actual*
January	57	100	60	75	57	100	60	75
February	160	110	150	100	217	210	210	175
March	62	75	75	140	279	285	285	315
April	175	150	150	120	454	435	435	435
May	550	400	500	520	1 004	835	935	955
June	475	525	525	500	1 479	1 360	1 460	1 455
July	560	550	575	600	2 039	1 910	2 035	2 055
August	205	200	175	200	2 244	2 110	2 210	2 255
September	490	525	475	450	2 734	2 635	2 685	2 705
October	710	690	725	710	3 444	3 325	3 410	3 415
November	390	450	400	350	3 834	3 775	3 810	3 765
December	120	130	150	200	3 954	3 905	3 960	3 965
TOTAL	3954	3905	3 960	3 965				

Comment

This chart has only one purpose: to warn chart makers and chart users away from the all-too-common error of packing an excessive amount of statistics on one chart. No matter how the legends or colors are arranged, the chart becomes useless when it is overcrowded. The solution is simple: use two charts. In this case prepare a factory chart and a separate distributor chart. Also, it is usually wise to separate monthly and year to date information. Sometimes they can appear on the same chart, but it becomes obvious quite readily that only the year to date performance versus budget is being used. Stay away from this type of chart; keep them simple and uncluttered.

Boat Division

CHART 3

MONTHLY 8 YEAR TO DATE UNIT SALES

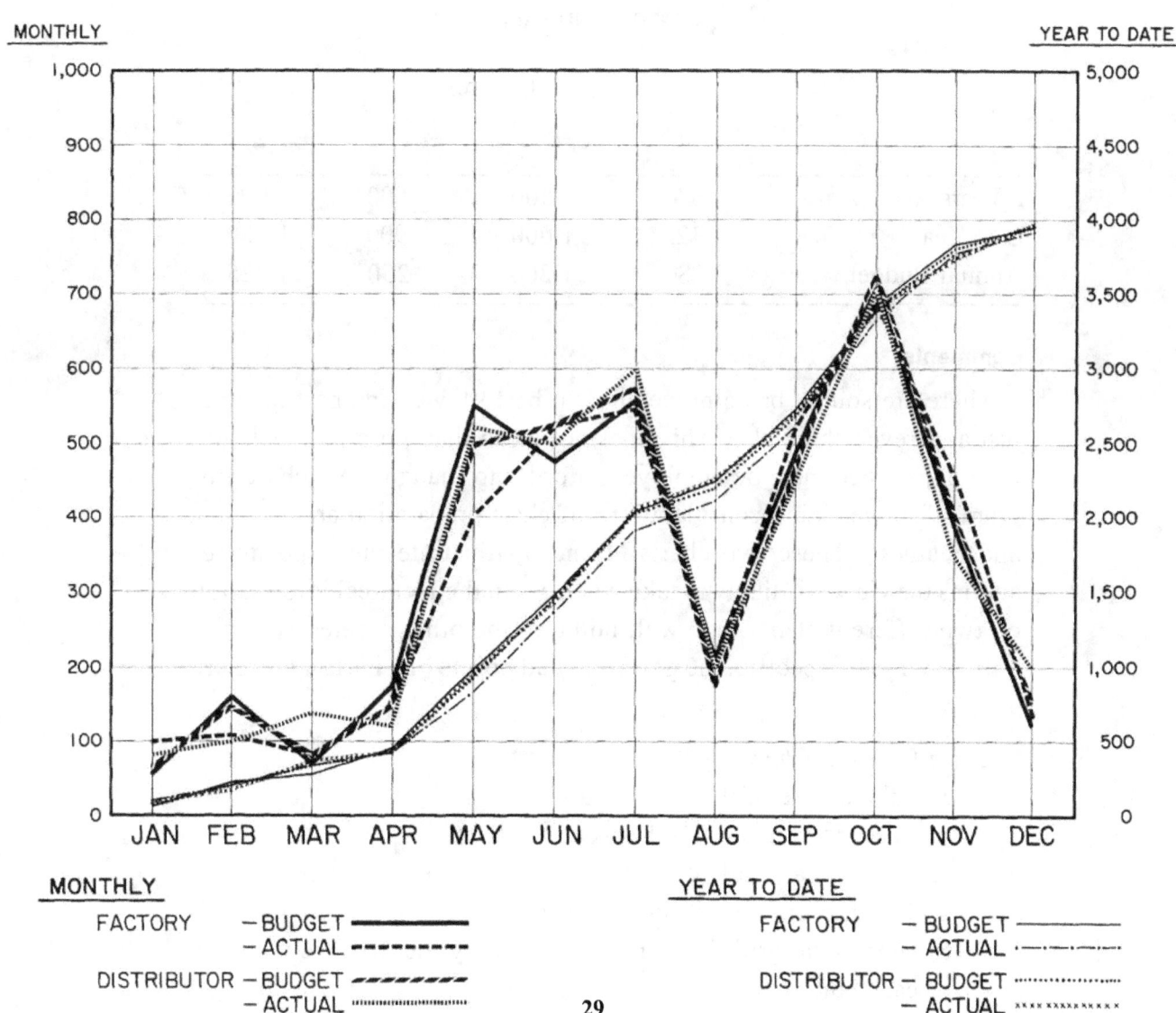

MONTHLY

			YEAR TO DATE
MONTHLY		YEAR TO DATE	
FACTORY	—BUDGET	FACTORY	—BUDGET
	—ACTUAL		—ACTUAL
DISTRIBUTOR	—BUDGET	DISTRIBUTOR	—BUDGET
	—ACTUAL		—ACTUAL

29

EXHIBIT FOR CHARTS 4 and 5

Actual Quarterly Unit Sales for the Last 2 Years and the Budget for This Year.

BOAT DIVISION

QUARTERLY UNIT SALES

	\multicolumn{4}{c}{Quarters}			
	1	2	3	4
2 Years Ago	300	1 500	800	1 000
Last Year	125	1 000	900	1 500
Annual Budget	280	1 200	1 250	1 225

Comments

There are sound, basic procedures to be followed in chart making, just as in everything else. This does not mean that a professional with long experience must be employed in order to inaugurate a chart program. The overriding considerations of chart preparation are accuracy and neatness. These two charts, 4 and 5, illustrate the opposite reactions the viewer is likely to take when given the identical information on two different charts, one well laid out, the other carelessly done.

In order to be specific, the good and bad points of Charts 4 and 5 are as follows:

Good Points in Chart 4
1. All bars are of the same width.
2. There is even spacing between the bars.
3. The bars are indented from the scale line.
4. The thickness of all lines is uniform.
5. Horizontal grid lines are used to easily identify the value of each bar.

CHART 4

Boat Division
QUARTERLY UNIT SALES

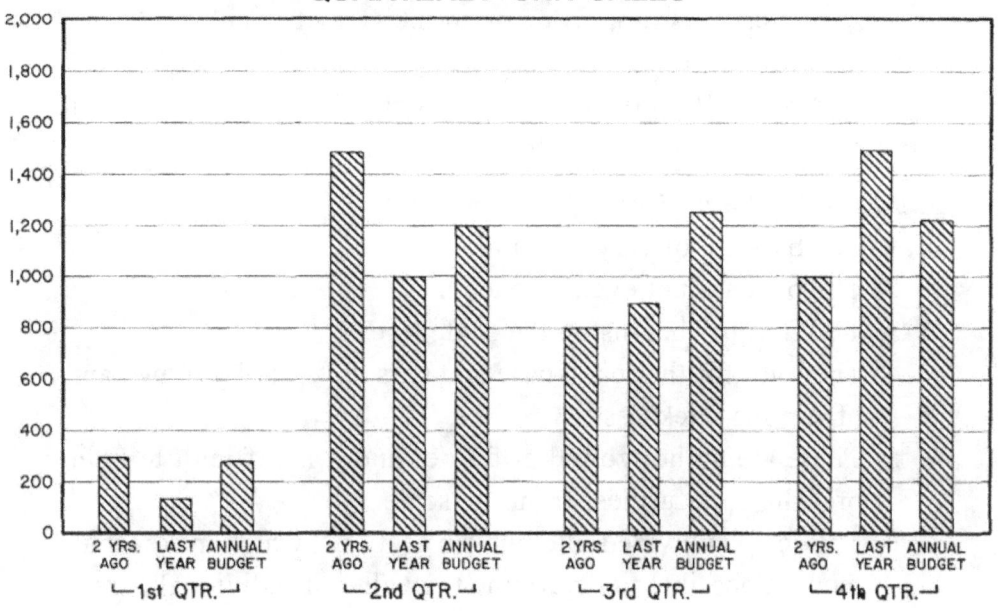

CHART 5

Boat Division
QUARTERLY UNIT SALES

6. The scale is divided into easily interpreted segments.
7. The title and all lettering is centered.
8. All lettering is proportionate to the size of the chart.
9. All lettering is neat and precise.
10. The over-all appearance of the chart is neat, "easy on the eyes" . . . it has a "professional" appearance.

Bad Points of Chart 5

1. The bars are of varying widths.
2. The bars are not evenly spaced.
3. The first bar begins on the scale line.
4. The lines for the scale, base and bars are sloppily drawn and of varying thickness.
5. There are no horizontal grid lines and it is difficult to interpret the bars furthest from the scale.
6. The scale is divided into uneven sections, which makes it almost impossible to determine the value of individual bars.
7. The title and other lettering is off center.
8. All lettering is too large and disproportionate to the requirements of the chart.
9. The lettering is carelessly done.
10. The chart is not boxed and the general appearance of the chart is messy and unattractive. It leads to the conclusion that charts are not an acceptable means of communication.

4

AUXILIARY AIDS TO GOOD CHARTS

The pictorial presentation of information can follow many basic patterns. In any given situation it should conform to the preference of the executive or management group using the charts. The author favors the simple-to-prepare, easy-to-understand type of chart.

This book illustrates a series of charts for a typical company. The major areas covered are sales, costs, profits, inventories, receivables, profit percent to sales, and return on assets. Examples of how these important management control items can be charted on an annual, quarterly, monthly, and cumulative basis occupy the major portion of the book. Additional approaches to data presentation which can augment the chart series are also discussed.

Slides

These can be in color or black and white. If slides are adopted the trend is usually to begin with black and white and then shift to color. Slides have a number of advantages and disadvantages. The advantages are:

1. Attractiveness.
2. Clarity of picture.
3. Easy to handle, transport and store.
4. Permanence.
5. Size of projected picture can be regulated.

Some of the disadvantages of slides are:

1. Costly.
2. Confidential material gets outside the company.
3. Requires a projector and screen.
4. Projection requires considerable space.
5. Long lead time required to prepare slides.
6. Changes cannot be made without preparing a new slide.

Direct Projection

There are a number of machines on the market which provide a simple means of projecting schedules of any kind. These use a direct projection technique in which the subject matter is placed in the machine and an enlarged picture appears on a screen.

The advantages of this form of presentation are:

1. No special preparation of documents is necessary.
2. Images can be any size for easy reading.
3. Clarity is guaranteed.
4. Projected image can be in black and white or color.
5. Easy to operate equipment.

The disadvantages of this technique are:

1. Requires a relatively dark room.
2. Cooling fan is noisy.
3. Projector and operator occupy a considerable area.
4. Poor definition of projected image from side viewing area.

Blackboards

These are portable and collapsible and generally range in size from 3' by 5' to 4' by 6'. They have overhead racks from which preprinted material can be suspended. This leaves the board itself free for use by the speaker. The slate can be cleaned with a special liquid which dries immediately. Slates are available in buff, pale green, black and ivory.

The advantages are:

1. Figures can be written as the speaker progresses.
2. The same board can be used for all types of presentations.
3. The figures can be cleanly erased and changes easily made.

There are several disadvantages:

1. The writing and erasing of figures may prove irritating and time consuming.
2. The writer is necessarily standing in front of part of his audience.
3. A large blackboard may prove awkward to store and transport.
4. The audience is restricted by its ability to see the figures being discussed.

Hand Lettered Schedules

An informal, 30" by 40" page can be used, on which pertinent information is usually written in ink or crayon. Special ink pens and crayons can be procured which produce large letters and numbers. The pages can be purchased in pads of 100 or more and hung on easels. As the discussion is completed the individual pages are turned, or looped over the back of the easel. This provides the informal name of "flop-over" charts. This means of presenting information has the following advantages:

1. The cost is minimal.
2. The schedules can be quickly prepared by any member of the staff.
3. A number of people can be preparing charts simultaneously.
4. Changes can be made by pasting a heavy white bond patch over the unwanted figure or word.
5. Additional pages can be added quickly.

The disadvantages are:

1. The charts are largely restricted to figures and text material.

2. They do not lend themselves to presenting trend information in line chart or bar chart form.
3. The charts cannot easily be updated.
4. Since they usually are restricted to current information, they must be used within a relatively short period of time.

There are a number of other forms of presentation as well as varied uses of the methods already described. However, the author feels that none of these begin to approach the inherent advantages of a well planned, complete and formalized system of charts which follow a basic pattern.

5

TEN PITFALLS TO BE AVOIDED

In any form of communication the greatest problem is getting everyone to interpret the data in the same way. While the impact of a visual presentation greatly overshadows a statistical schedule or an interpretive text, there are a number of pitfalls to avoid in preparing charts. It is possible to have a number of people receive completely different impressions of what is most significant when looking at an improperly prepared chart. It is essential that those reading the charts, as well as those responsible for preparing them, be aware of the most common faults of poor charts.

Some examples of the more outstanding misinterpretations are:

1. *Comparative Size of Figures*

A very common chart shows population changes. These are often illustrated by having a man two inches tall and two inches wide represent 20 million or some other basic number of people. When the population doubles, the man would be expected to be four inches tall and two inches wide. However, in many cases the figure is drawn four inches high and four inches wide, creating the impression that the population is four times the base total instead of two times.

2. *Disproportionate Scales*

It is not always possible to compare the operations of several product lines on the same chart. The alternative is to draw two charts and

37

place them side by side. It is deceiving to employ two different scales in making this comparison. For instance, a product line with sales of $100 million will look larger than a product line with $200 million if the first scale runs from zero to $100 million and the second scale is drawn from zero to $600 million. Both scales should be drawn to a common maximum. The wrong technique is clearly demonstrated by Chart 6.

3. *Dual Scales*

The use of two scales on one chart should be avoided wherever possible. However, receivable and inventory charts bring the story into sharper focus when both the dollar balances and the number of day's, week's or month's sales are on the same chart. In these cases the dollar scale should be on the left and the number of days, weeks or months scale should be on the right. The two scales should be different in height, the scale numbers should differ in color, and the legend for each scale should be clearly marked at the top. The proper technique appears on Chart 44, Chapter 11, dealing with receivables. It is also demonstrated by the series of weekly and monthly sales charts which include year to date information.

4. *Inconsistent Base Lines*

The most difficult charts to interpret are those with base lines which do not begin with zero. The entire chart is thrown out of proportion if a chart has a maximum scale of $20 million and the base line represents $4 million. This is illustrated by Chart 7. There are, of course, logical exceptions to charting rules, just as there are to most other procedures. A base line other than zero can be very effective for plotting company sales as a percent of industry. Suppose, for example, that a firm has always had more than 10 per cent of industry sales in a particular product line, but in the foreseeable future it will not exceed 20 per cent. It is both informative and practical to have a scale from 10 to 20 per cent, so that fluctuations can be accentuated, especially when one full percentage change either way has a significant effect on profits.

Under these circumstances a scale from zero to 20 per cent would minimize and obscure important variations which should be brought to the management's attention.

It is recommended that in those cases where a chart cannot accommodate an unusually wide range of statistics the chart be broken at some logical point in the scale. This approach is shown in Chart 8. It is equally important that a zero base line be clearly marked when both profits and losses appear on the same chart. In these instances the zero line should be unusually heavy and the loss portion of the scale should be shown in red. The recommended solution to showing profits and losses on the same chart is demonstrated by Chart 4. When it is not possible, because of duplicating limitations, to show the losses in red, they should be identified with a legend or by indicating that the section below the line is the loss area. The recommended technique is to clearly mark the profit section and the loss section in the left hand margin of the chart, as shown on Chart 9.

5. *Run Figures Off Chart*

Do not allow figures to run off the top or bottom of the chart, if at all possible. In some cases the range of data is so extreme that the chart cannot properly accommodate it. In these instances indicate by the use of figures the amount which would have been plotted had space permitted. An example of this appears in Chart 5.

6. *No Indication of Values Being Plotted*

There is no excuse for the chart user having to guess at the values shown on a chart. Through the employment of adequate headings, scales, grid lines, numbers on the top or inside of bars, etc., the information being plotted should be quickly and easily discernible.

7. *Lack of Subject Identification*

Room should be provided at the top of every chart to identify the information being presented. This identity should include the firm name, division, subject matter such as sales, profits, ratios, etc., the units of value such as dollars, pounds, whether the values are expressed in thousands, millions, etc., and the time periods being covered. The charts for the Francis Company in later chapters of this book consistently follow this rule.

8. *Repeating Standard Information*

If a division or a department is presenting charts to its own management, it may be unnecessary to repeat the division or department name on every chart. However, when comparisons are made with other operating units, the names of both units must appear and be identified with the material being plotted. This same omission is possible to some degree in other areas, but is considered dangerous and may lead to confusion and misinterpretation. It should be noted that in the later chapters the Francis Company title appears on every chart. In the forward section of the book the lettered charts have no company name; these alternate approaches must be adapted to specific circumstances and the preference of the chart supervisor and users.

9. *Plot on Scale Line*

Information should not be plotted on the vertical line which represents the scale. All data on the left or right sides of a chart should be indented from the scale line. The incorrect method is shown on Chart 11 and Chart 5. The correct procedure appears on all other charts in this book.

10. *Lack of Scale Planning*

The basic purpose of a chart is to present information clearly and concisely. Charts with improper scales cannot be understood. The scales must use normally accepted variations such as 2-4-6-8-10, or 5-10-15-20, etc., or 10-20-30-40. Unacceptable scales are those which show 7-14-21-28, etc. or 13-26-39-52, etc. These are difficult to understand and destroy the utility of the chart. Examples of incorrect scale designations appear on Chart 5.

CHARTS 6 THROUGH 11

EXHIBIT FOR LINE CHART 6

Actual Sales for the Past 5 Years

TRUCK SALES

LAST 5 YEARS

	Top	Bottom
	Chart	Chart
($ Millions)		
5 Years Ago	15	75
4 Years Ago	27	115
3 Years Ago	40	150
2 Years Ago	75	180
Last Year	95	200

Comments

Two entirely different sets of statistics are presented exactly the same way on two line charts. The purpose is to show the deception which can be employed using charts; unfortunately all media lend themselves to misinterpretation unless extreme care is exercised. In this instance a great deal of harm can result if scales are not carefully selected when making comparisons. When this affects the evaluation of one person's ability as a manager versus another's performance, it becomes very serious.

In the top chart the use of a small scale makes it appear the manager is doing an outstanding job of selling product over a 5-year period, and that the individual responsible for the sales shown in the lower section of chart 6 has made very little progress. Actually, the gain in sales in the top chart has been only $80 million, but in the bottom chart sales have gone up $125 million.

The author recommends careful consideration be given to scale selection and the purpose of the comparisons. This understanding should be as much the responsibility of the chart reviewer as the chart maker.

Truck Sales

CHART 6

LAST 5 YEARS

($ MILLIONS)

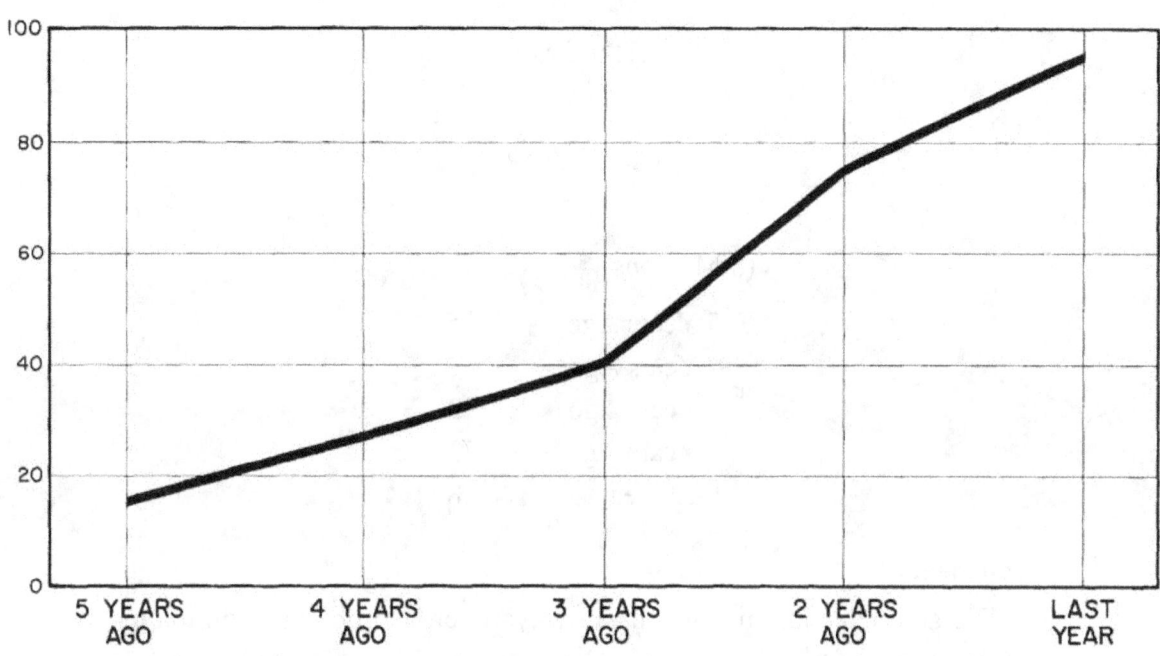

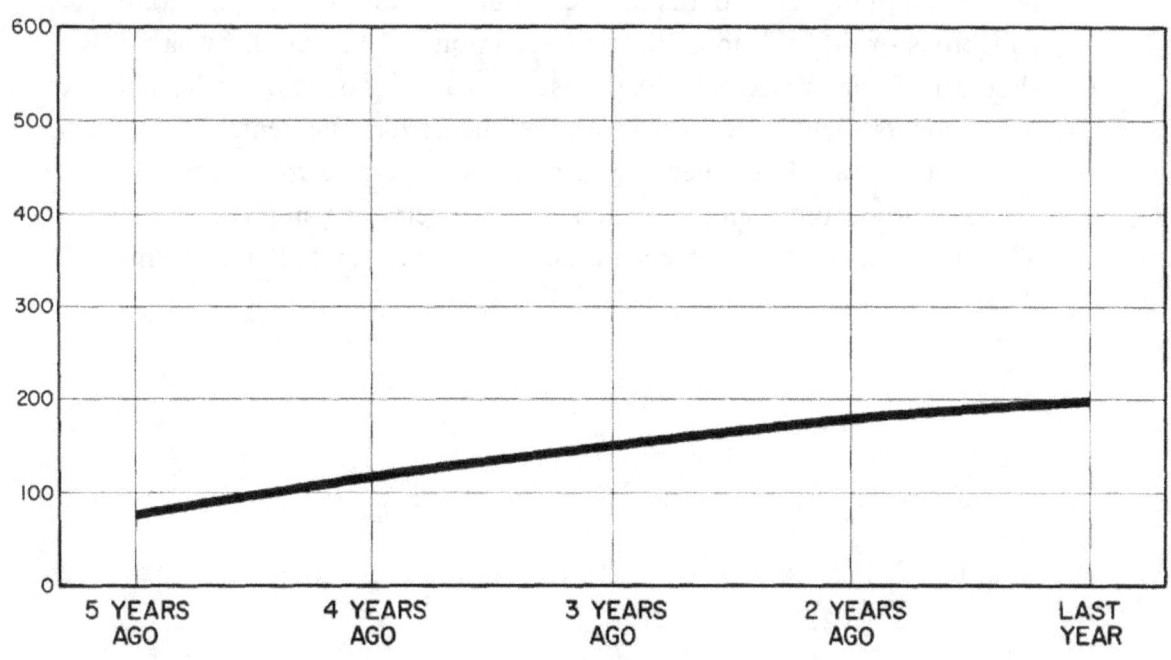

EXHIBIT FOR LINE CHART 7

Actual Sales for Last 5 Years

TIRE SALES

LAST 5 YEARS

($ Millions)

5 Years Ago	5
4 Years Ago	8
3 Years Ago	12
2 Years Ago	13
Last Year	18

Comments

The art of communication has always been a problem within companies and between companies. The chart techniques described in this book attempt to set standards for clearer understandings and illustrate dangerous or difficult to understand techniques. The data for Chart 7 should not be shown except with the use of a base line of zero. Dollar and unit amounts should *always* have a base line of zero. Percentages may begin with a base line other than zero *if* the departure from normally accepted procedure is clearly understood by everyone using the charts. The author always recommends a zero base line for dollar and unit data.

Tire Sales

CHART 7

LAST 5 YEARS
($ MILLIONS)

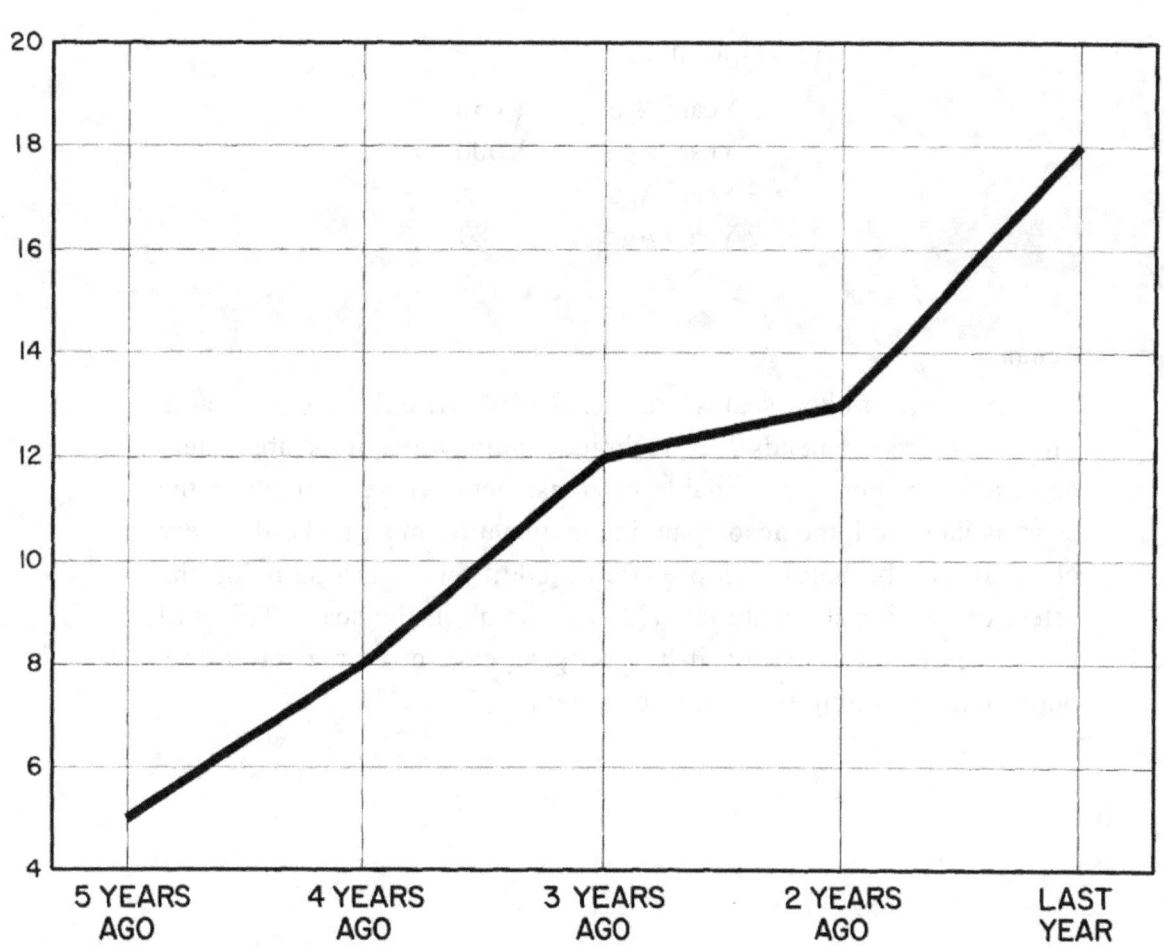

EXHIBIT FOR LINE CHART 8

Actual Sales for Last 5 Years

ICE BOX SALES

LAST 5 YEARS

($ Thousands)

5 Years Ago	1 050
4 Years Ago	1 000
3 Years Ago	100
2 Years Ago	80
Last Year	75

Comments

Charts with broken scales are sometimes difficult to understand. The author recommends this technique only when it is absolutely necessary. In those unavoidable circumstances where a break in the chart is indicated, the accompanying explanation must make this very clear. It may be helpful to prepare an additional chart showing the effect of plotting the material without a break in the scale. This will put the entire presentation in the proper perspective and provide a better understanding by all the reviewers.

Ice Box Sales

LAST 5 YEARS

($ THOUSANDS)

CHART 8

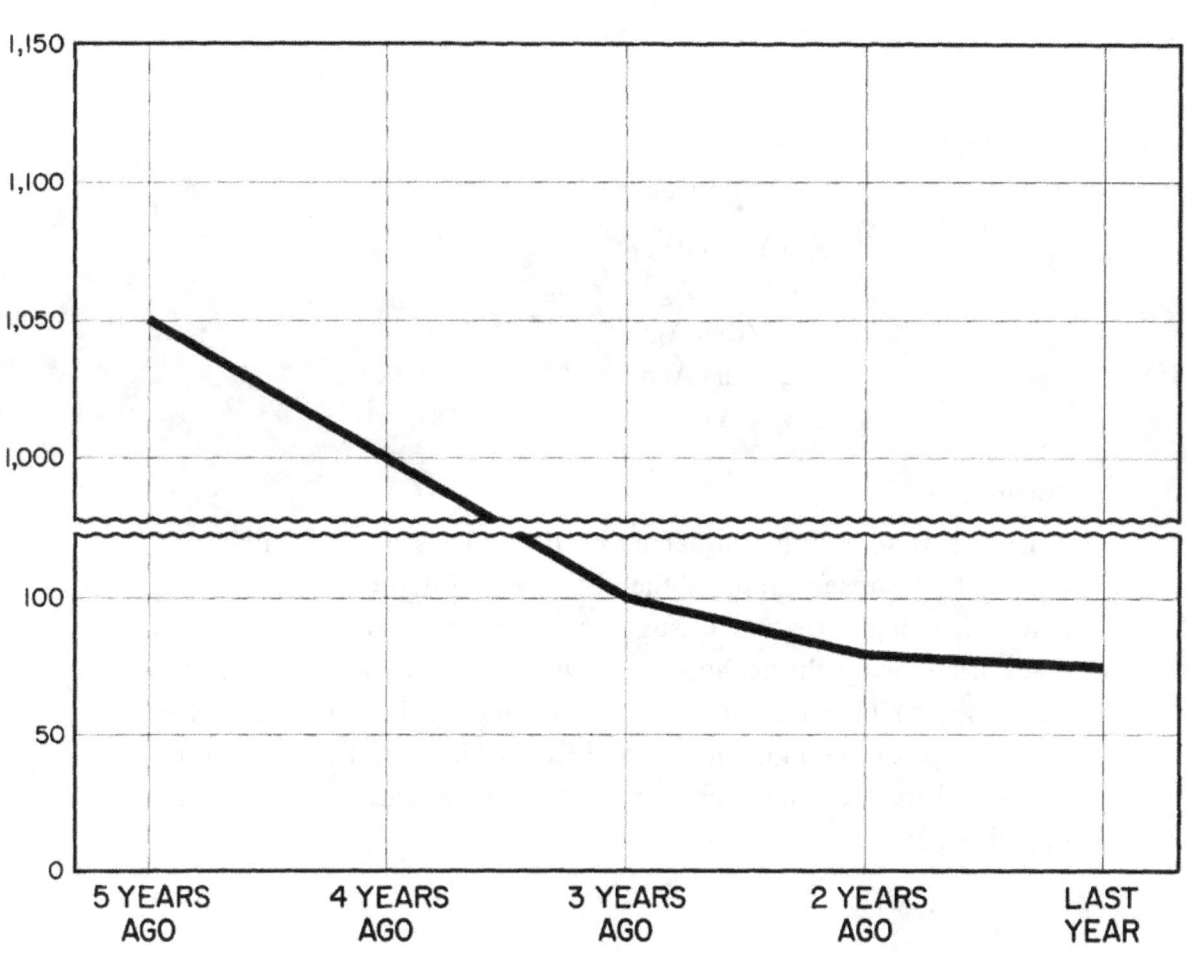

EXHIBIT FOR LINE CHART 9

Actual Profits and (Losses) for Last 5 Years

ICE BOX PROFITS

LAST 5 YEARS

($ Thousands)

5 Years Ago	80
4 Years Ago	50
3 Years Ago	2
2 Years Ago	(5)
Last Year	(8)

Comments

This chart shows how to handle profits and losses. The author recommends the reservation of the color red to depict losses. Where colors cannot be used, it is suggested that the loss area be clearly marked either by the technique shown or by indicating within the chart itself which is the "profit area" and which is the "loss area." Note that the type of line in the loss area differs from the solid line used for profits. There are a number of acceptable techniques; all that is required is clarity.

Ice Box Profits

CHART 9

LAST 5 YEARS

($ THOUSANDS)

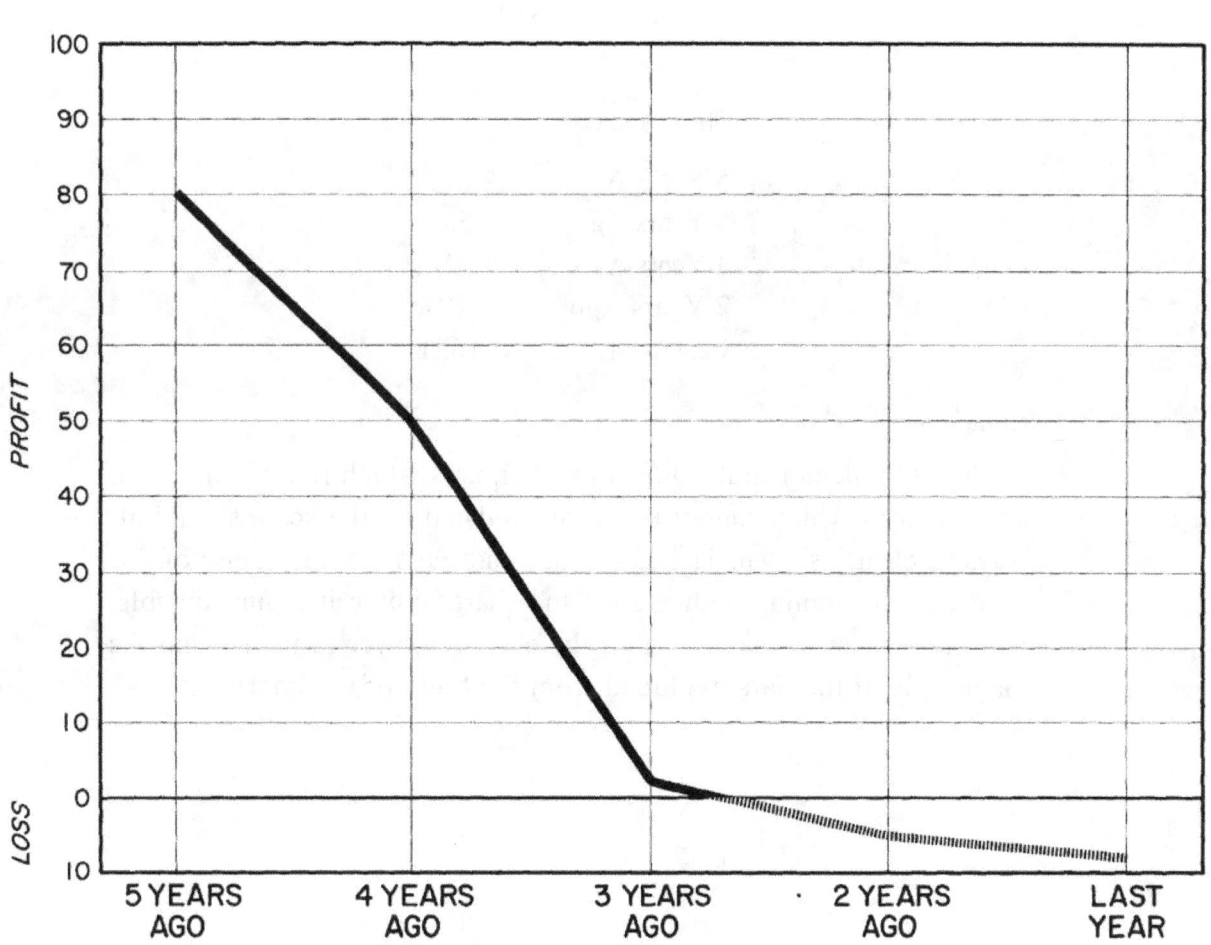

EXHIBIT FOR LINE CHART 10

Actual Profits and (Losses) for Last 5 Years

ICE BOX PROFITS LAST 5 YEARS

AND NEXT YEAR

($ Thousands)

5 Years Ago	80
4 Years Ago	50
3 Years Ago	2
2 Years Ago	(8)
Last Year	(62)

Comments

This chart demonstrates how to plot figures which run off the chart. The amounts which cannot be accommodated by the scale should always be clearly shown. The author does not favor extensive use of this procedure of running numbers off the chart. Where it is unavoidable, great care must be taken to alert the chart reviewer to its use and the magnitude of the data excluded from the body of the chart.

Ice Box Profits

CHART 10

LAST 5 YEARS

($ THOUSANDS)

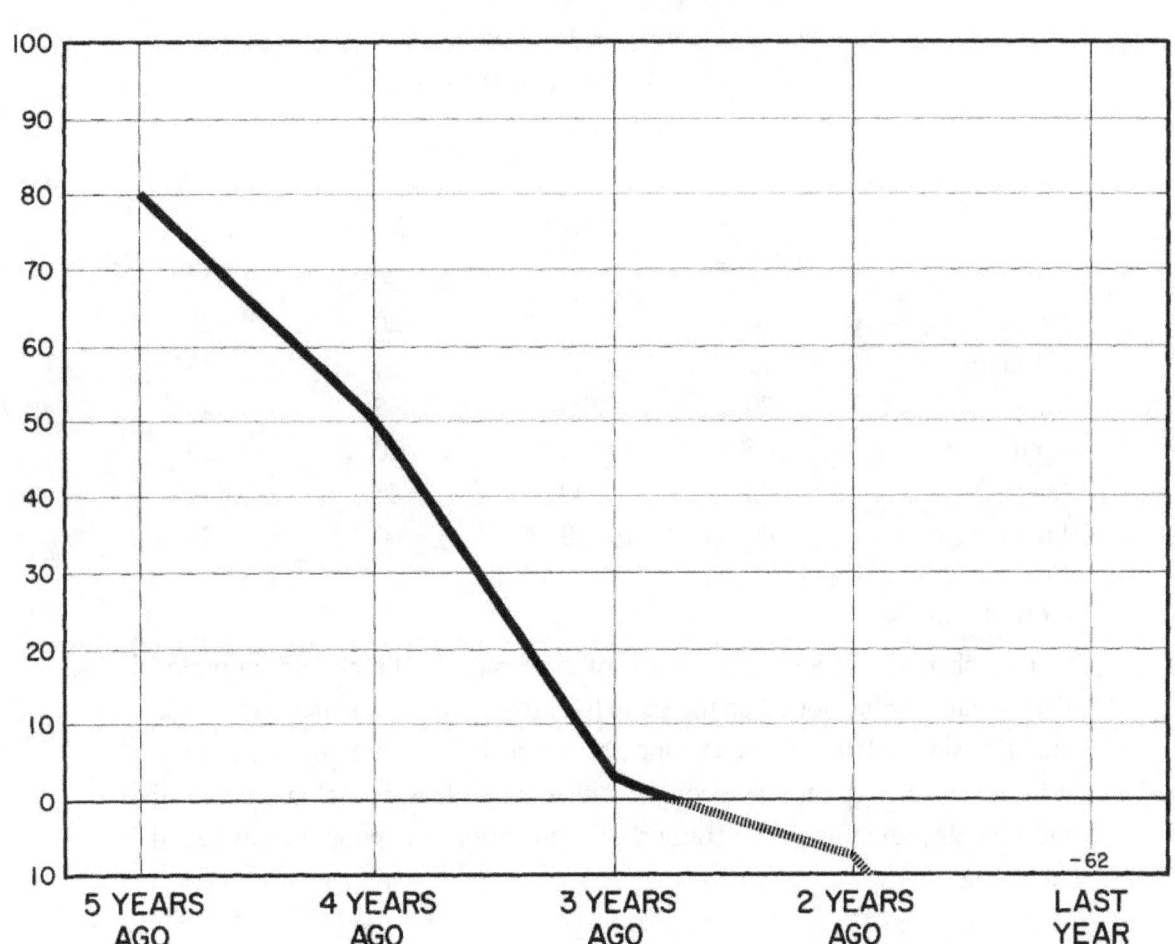

	5 YEARS AGO	4 YEARS AGO	3 YEARS AGO	2 YEARS AGO	LAST YEAR

EXHIBIT FOR LINE CHART 11

Actual Cumulative Monthly Unit Sales for This Year

BICYCLE DIVISION VERSUS COMPETITORS

CUMULATIVE MONTHLY UNIT SALES

THIS YEAR

	Bicycle Division	*Fast Co.*	*Rapid Co.*	*Speed Co.*
January	10	15	20	25
February	15	20	30	35
March	20	25	35	40
April	25	30	40	50
May	30	40	45	60
June	40	50	60	85

Comments

This chart shows a common error of preparation. The beginning period data should *not* be plotted on the scale line. It should be indented to the right and left sides of the chart, leaving the vertical lines free for scales. The information can be just as accurate either way. This is not a matter of individual preference, but rather an indication of poor versus good technique.

CHART 11

Bicycle Division vs. Competitors
CUMULATIVE MONTHLY UNIT SALES
THIS YEAR

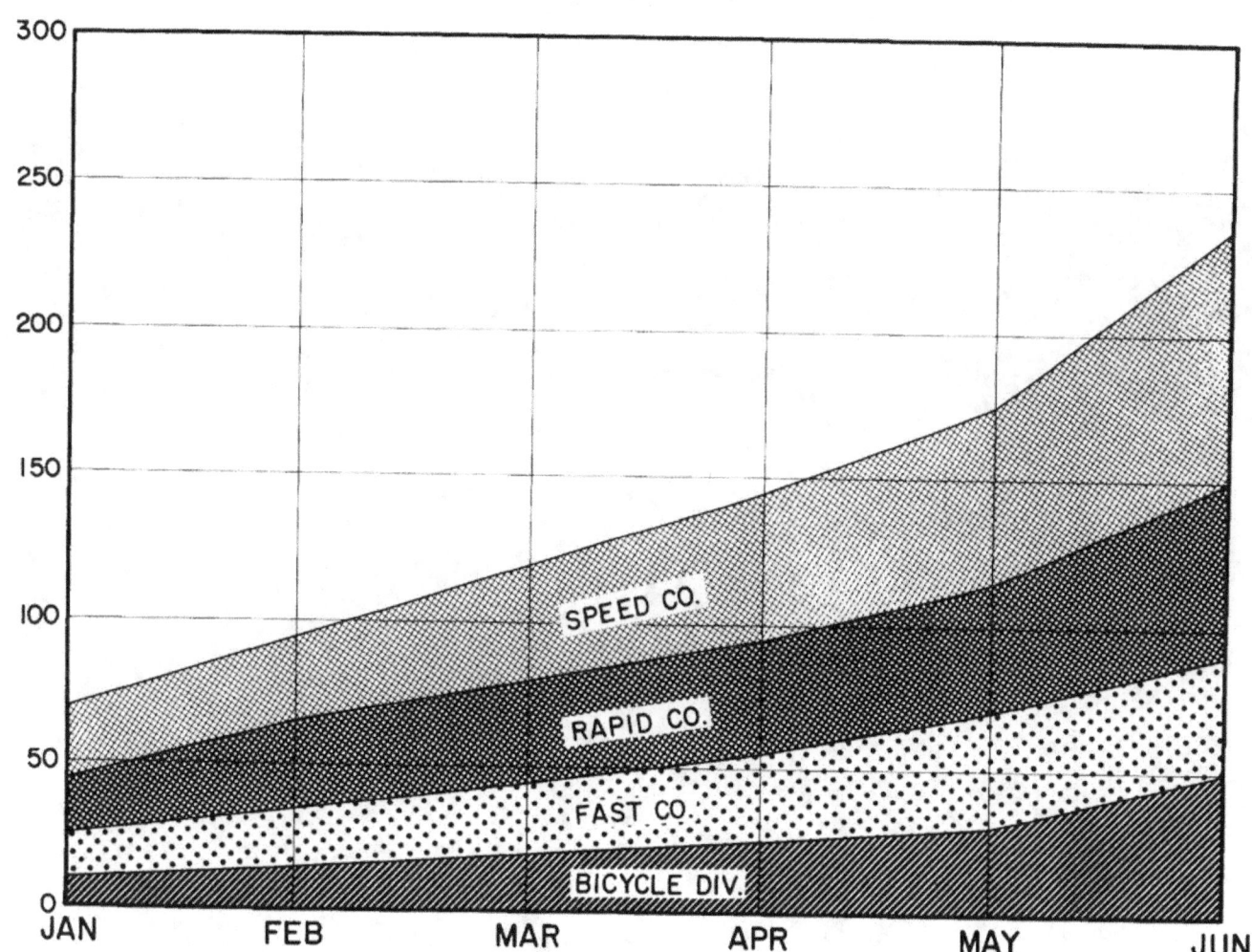

6

PRACTICAL CHART PROCEDURE

Chart Personnel

A well rounded chart program serves all normal and special corporate staff requirements, plus occasional work for operating divisions. The staff at corporate headquarters may consist of a chart supervisor, one full time chartist and an accountant who gathers the necessary statistics, transcribes them to the standard chart forms and checks the charts before they are released for reproduction and distribution. The accountant may devote about 50 per cent of his time to chart work.

Chart Supervisor

It is, naturally, impossible to outline a step-by-step approach to a complete chart program which will answer every question in all companies. In the large, diversified organization, a sizeable financial staff is usually available and the person in charge of the chart program may be in the financial analysis section, the controller's department, the treasurer's office, etc. In the small and medium size company, where a relatively few people in the accounting function handle nearly all special projects, the problem of selection will probably narrow down to one or two people. However, a sound general principle to follow is this: select an individual who is the "idea" type, who can analyze data quickly and has the ability to grasp the over-all approach to problems and sell an idea to the management. A chart program is more than drawing lines on graph paper. It must tell an effective story. It must be practical. It must be accepted and used by all levels of management. For these obvious reasons the chart program supervisor must not be relegated to a minor role if the investment is going to pay off.

Chartist

The person should have a background in mechanical drawing or commercial art in order to produce the most effective chart. In addition to this type of training the individual should be creative and demonstrate an ability to visualize a well balanced chart prior to the actual layout and drawing. He must have the ability to balance headings, scales, time periods and descriptive material so the chart has a "professional" appearance. There is no question that an accurate chart will tell the same story without all these refinements, but the message seems a bit more difficult to decipher when the picture is "out of focus." The chartist requires no accounting or statistical training. It is necessary, however, to make certain that his instructions are kept simple and clear and are consistently presented.

Statistician

The person supplying the statistics to be plotted should have a knowledge of accounting, in order to make certain the financial data represents the facts and is being fairly presented. The person must also have the ability to check the accuracy of the chart against the statistical data and be able to recognize errors in headings, scales and explanatory information. In other words, a high degree of accuracy and perception is required.

Company Needs

Once the chart supervisor has been selected, an analysis of the company's needs should begin. As pointed out in Chapter 2, there are two basic approaches to a full-scale program. The first, and usually the best, method is to complete a series of charts on total company operations. This can be followed by charting divisional and subsidiary results, historically and for the future. The determination of what charts to use should be the result of a coordinated effort on the part of the chart supervisor, the controller, the people in charge of issuing statistical information and the various management levels who will use the charts. This latter group should include the president plus the heads of the sales, manufacturing, marketing, advertising, purchasing and administrative departments. Not only should there be complete under-standing of the charts which affect the individual departments and activities, but all responsible personnel should have an appreciation of the total company concept. It will be most educational for all members of the management team to review total results, plus the charts dealing with each phase of the operation. These initial and continuing reviews will produce an awareness of the other person's responsibilities and problems.

Chart Materials

When the first set of plans has been drawn depicting the basic charts for sales, profits, costs and expenses by years, quarters, months and weeks, the company is ready to consider the chart materials re-quired.

The following is an approximate inventory of the chart equipment and supplies which are considered essential for a basic program. Also included are supplementary materials for use in a more elaborate pro-gram which will include special assignments.

Basic Requirements

    Drafting Table
    T-Square
    12" Engineer's Scale
    18" Triangle
    Electric Eraser
    Ruling Pen
    Ink Compass
    Basic Mechanical Lettering Set
    Various Color Drawing Inks
    Pen Cleaning Kit
    Masking Tape
    22" by 30" 3-Ply Chart Board

Additional Special Supplies

      Parallel Straight Edge
      24" Engineer's Scale
      Various Size Triangles
      Drafting Instrument Set
      Complete Mechanical Lettering Set
      Various Style Mechanical Lettering Guides such as: Gothic, Old
         English, Script, etc.
      Transparent Shading Sheets
      Various Color and Size Chart Tape
      Various Rapid Design Templates
      Percentage Protractor
      Plastic Burnisher
      X-Acto Knife
      Plastic Curves
      Various Size Lettering Pens
      Large Paper Cutter
      Tracing Box
      Tabouret
      Rubber Cement
      Various Size Illustration Board
      Cellulose Acetate Sheets

Statistical Chart Schedule

The chartist should be given a standard statistical format containing the detail required to prepare a series of charts on such activities as sales, net profits, per cent to sales, fixed assets, total assets, per cent return on assets, etc. The division or product line name should be shown at the top. Additional information would include whether these are line charts or bar charts and an indication of the maximum limits of the scale for each chart. The chartist should know in advance what color to use for sales, profits, etc. throughout the company. For example, sales can be black, profits green, losses red, etc. Where it is impractical to use colors, a distinct legend should be assigned to each major item such as sales, profits, assets, and so on. Suggestions are listed in Chapter 3.

A statistical format used for plotting annual data is shown below.

It would be the same for weekly, monthly or quarterly charts except the left-hand column would specify the exact time periods.

NAME OF DIVISION OR PRODUCT LINE
LINE CHART

($ in Thousands)

Time Period	Sales	Net Profit	% Profit to Sales	Fixed Assets	Total Assets	% Return on Assets
Last Year						
This Year						
Next Year						
2 Years						
3 Years						
4 Years						
5 Years						

Charting Procedure

The following steps encompass the normal chart cycle from beginning to end. This covers both regular weekly and monthly charts and special chart requests.

1. The chart supervisor recommends the charts needed to carry out the regular series required by the executive management. He also re views special charts requested by the management and fits these into the timing schedule. In addition the supervisor consults with those in charge of the divisional chart programs, on format, content, number, selection of material and personnel, layout of the chart room and up dating.

2. The chartist recommends the layout of each chart consistent with the standard format adopted for scales, headings, time periods and types of charts. He then prepares the basic outline, plots the figures and turns the completed chart over to the accountant for checking.

3. The accountant obtains almost all statistical information from regularly published financial statements. In some instances, special studies are conducted on a particular phase of a company operation

and this data is translated into a special chart or chart series. In these cases, the completed report will contain the chart, the supporting figures and interpretive comments.

After checking the chart plottings against the data supplied to the chartist, the accountant releases the master chart to the photostat department for reproduction, usually in 8½ by 11 inch sizes. The original charts are usually prepared in one of three sizes, 8½ by 11, or 20 by 30 or 30 by 40 inches.

When the charts have been reproduced, they are distributed as follows:

First, a set is sent to the Financial Vice President and another set goes to the Vice President and Controller for review and approval.

Second, after approval is received, the original chart is hung in the chart room.

Third, sets are distributed to the corporate staff and divisional people whose operation has been charted. For example, if the charts concern television receivers, the Executive Vice President in charge of consumer products receives a set, along with the Vice President and General Manager, the Controller and the Administrative Director of the Television Division.

Finally, these charts are updated weekly if they contain weekly data, monthly if they reflect monthly financial results, quarterly in some cases or perhaps annually if they contain only 12 months information or are comparisons with competitors. It should be the responsibility of the chart supervisor to lay out and maintain a schedule of updating.

A series of charts can be prepared which demonstrate to the management how weekly, monthly, quarterly and annual charts can be presented as line charts, bar charts or pie charts.

The author feels that the use of line charts versus bar charts is usually a matter of individual preference, rather than the superior characteristics of one chart type over the other providing that the charts are kept simple and are not overcrowded. When a maximum of data or a number of comparisons are desired on a single chart, the line chart is probably best. In order to demonstrate this, the same data for unit sales is plotted on a series of line charts and bar charts in this chapter. These sample charts show unit sales for purposes of illustration only. The same technique and format can apply to dollars of profit, manufacturing costs, general and administrative expenses, etc.

Line Charts

Samples of line charts for sales are shown on subsequent pages, and are identified as follows:

Sample Line Charts for Unit Sales

Weekly............................ Chart 12
Monthly .... Chart 13
Quarterly........................ Chart 14
Annually .... Chart 15
Combined Annual and
    Quarterly .... Chart 16

Weekly—Chart 12. This chart demonstrates a technique in which a sales plan is plotted using the left-hand scale for weekly data, while cumulative or year to date information is plotted against the right-hand scale. Two things must be made very clear when using this technique.

1. There must be no mistaking the fact that the left scale represents weekly information and that the right scale reflects annual or year to date figures.

2. The two scales must complement each other in easily determined multiples. For example, if the left scale goes to a height of 2,000, the right scale should go to 4,000, 20,000, 40,000, etc. using multiples of 2, 20, etc. The right scale should not go to 5,000, 50,000, etc. where different multiples of 2.5, 25, etc. must be plotted. This is often over looked and leads to a chart which is extremely unwieldy and difficult to use.

A distinction should be made between estimates and actual results through the use of colors or legends. This same technique can be applied, to weekly production and other types of information.

Monthly—Chart 13. This is one type of chart for plotting the sales effect of lower or higher prices, special promotions, increased area coverage, licensing additional distributors, increasing the number of models in the line, etc. It is, of course, necessary to clearly label the effect of each of the several courses of action. It is recommended that distinctive labels be used instead of legends, in order to avoid confusion by those reviewing this type of chart. If a line chart is used for illustrating the results of alternate courses of action, the number of alternates must be kept to a minimum. *This restricts the utility of a line chart for this type of presentation and favors a bar chart, as shown on Chart 18.*

Quarterly—Chart 14. These charts are used most frequently for comparing product lines affected by sharp seasonal swings. It is recommended that these be restricted to comparisons of a number of prior years, and possibly an evaluation of the forecasting trend in the coming year. It is often possible, with this type of chart, to detect a change in the sales department philosophy, in which they forecast a shift in peak volume from the normal pattern into an earlier or later quarter. By investigating such changes in the projections, the management can quickly become aware of forecasting errors, new promotional plans or perhaps a sales department policy which does not coincide with other company programs. *This chart is not as easy to follow as Bar Chart 19.*

Annually—Chart 15. These are basic charts which should clearly reflect long term trends versus short and long range plans. It is suggested that line charts can perform a most useful service if this type of chart goes back five years and forward five years. It will not only reveal whether sales are going up, down or have plateaued, but it places a five-year plan in the proper perspective. For example, if sales have shown a steady year-by-year decline, there would be a serious question about the company's ability to precipitate a steep upswing within the next few years. It would certainly be unwise to plan an expense structure to meet an optimistic outlook without a detailed analysis of the sales plan.

It is, of course, also possible on this type of chart to show the effect of new products or new merchandising methods on the sales curve. When these alternate plans are plotted, the sales chart should always be accompanied by the others in the standard series of charts, namely, the profits, the assets required, the profit per cent to sales and the per cent return on assets.

Combined Annual and Quarterly—Chart 16. In this chart the management can determine both the annual trend over a period of years plus the quarterly behavior pattern. It is recommended that the annual section be shown first and that the quarters be grouped individually by years. For instance, if five years of history are going to be plotted, these annual statistics would be to the left side of the chart, using a scale to accommodate the peak year. The next element to the right of the annual plottings would be a scale for the quarterly data. Immediately to the right of the quarterly scale would be the first quarter, with each year plotted in the same sequence used in the annual data section. The next group of plottings would show the second quarter results for each of the years, and so on with the third and fourth quarter. *This information is more easily interpreted on Bar Chart 21.*

Bar Charts

The line charts which have previously been illustrated are being repeated on subsequent pages for comparative purposes. In other words, the sample line charts 12 through 16 for unit sales will be shown as 17 through 21 as bar charts. These sample bar charts will be identified as follows:

Sample Bar Charts for Unit Sales

Weekly .... Chart 17
Monthly .... Chart 18
Quarterly .... Chart 19
Annually .... Chart 20
Combined Annually
    and Quarterly .... Chart 21

Weekly—Chart 17. In plotting both weekly and year to date information on a bar chart it is necessary to use two charts; it is impractical to attempt plotting weekly, monthly or quarterly data on a chart which also contains cumulative statistics. For this reason, Line Chart 12 must be represented by two bar charts, 17 for the weekly data and 17A for the cumulative unit sales. *This points out a practical limitation of the bar chart, and emphasizes the advantages of a line chart.*

It is important to make certain that whatever system is adopted regarding weekly versus cumulative, annual versus quarterly, etc., scales be followed consistently on all chart presentations, both at the total company and divisional level. It is suggested that rules such as this, plus the assignment of colors and legends to different items be written and made available to all those having chart responsibility throughout the company.

Monthly—Chart 18. This chart is helpful in illustrating the monthly trend of sales for one or two years. It is also excellent for plotting a number of alternate courses of action. *While this chart contains the same information depicted by sample line Chart 13, it is much easier to use.* Instead of having the bars next to each other, the impact of each course of action could be demonstrated by building one segment on top of another. This is a matter of individual preference.

Quarterly—Chart 19. This type of chart lends itself to a grouping of data for a period of years. It sharpens the changes in sales for each quarter and also highlights the relative importance of a series of quarters by years. Although it is strictly a matter of individual preference, *the author feels that a bar chart for quarterly data is much superior to the same information illustrated by line chart 14.*

Annually—Chart 20. The practical value of this chart depends upon the purpose to be served. If it is used to show a long range picture, such as five years of history and five or 10 years ahead, it is excellent, and is highly recommended. It does not lend itself to indicating the effect of alternate courses of action, unless the user is able to understand that as each section of a bar is added, it reflects an increase over and above the total effect of all other courses of action. To do this, the bars must be distinctly labelled, but the problem of evaluating the many segments of the bars is still difficult.

Combined Annually and Quarterly—Chart 21. This type of chart can be very effective. It produces an annual trend to the left and then highlights each quarter by years, and at the same time compares the relative importance of each quarter to the year's total results. *The author strongly recommends this chart over a similar line type presentation in Chart 16.* It is most important, however, in constructing this type of chart, to emphasize the difference in scales. The scale to the left depicts total annual figures. To the right of the annual data a scale must appear which relates to the quarterly information. It is sometimes advisable to have the annual scale line extend higher on the chart than the quarterly scale line. This denotes a larger quantity, in addition to the disparity in scale values.

Pie Charts

This type of chart is probably seen most often in corporate reports to stockholders to illustrate the splitting of the sales dollar. Its outstanding feature is the clarity with which it fragments pieces of data. *This type of chart Hs not recommended to compete with the sample line or bar charts contained in this chapter.* If necessary, the pie chart could be employed to show annual sales in relationship to a 5 or 10 year total; profits and other data could be handled in the same manner. However, since line charts and bar charts portray this type of information so much more clearly, the pie chart must be considered to have a somewhat specialized and restricted value.

Some idea of how a pie chart might be used for product line presentations is shown on sample charts 22 and 23. Pie chart 22 shows dollar sales of various product lines adding to the company total. Pie chart 23 shows the dollar profits for these same product lines and the per cent of each product line profit to total profits. This comparison indicates, to a general extent, how one product line, with relatively small dollar volume contributes a disproportionate share of the total dollar profits.

A further refinement of either the unit or per cent technique using pie charts is possible. This is through the use of acetate overlays. One chart—for example, the profit chart—can be placed on top of the sales chart and the relative importance of each product line is easily evaluated. This is an especially effective procedure when discussing a sales and profit relationship with one person or a small group of people and the charts can be placed on a flat surface.

EXHIBIT FOR LINE CHART 12 AND BAR CHART 17
Actual and Budgeted Weekly and Year to Date Unit Sales

BOAT DIVISION

UNIT SALES

WEEKLY AND YEAR TO DATE

ACTUAL VERSUS PLAN

	Plan			Actual	
		Year to			*Year to*
	Week	*Date*		*Week*	*Date*
1/9	10	10		25	25
1/16	12	22		20	45
1/23	15	37		30	75
1/30	20	57		15	90
2/ 6	30	87		10	100
2/13	40	127		20	120
2/20	60	187		50	170
2/27	30	217		60	230
3/ 6	15	232		40	270
3/13	12	244		25	295
3/20	15	259		50	345
3/27	20	279		60	405
4/ 3	25	304			
4/10	35	339			
4/17	50	389			
4/24	65	454			
5/ 1	75	529			
5/ 8	100	629			
5/15	150	779			
5/22	125	904			
5/29	100	1 004			
6/ 5	150	1 154			
6/12	100	1 254			
6/17	75	1 329			
6/26	150	1 479			

CHART 12

Boat Division
WEEKLY & YEAR TO DATE UNIT SALES
ACTUAL vs. PLAN

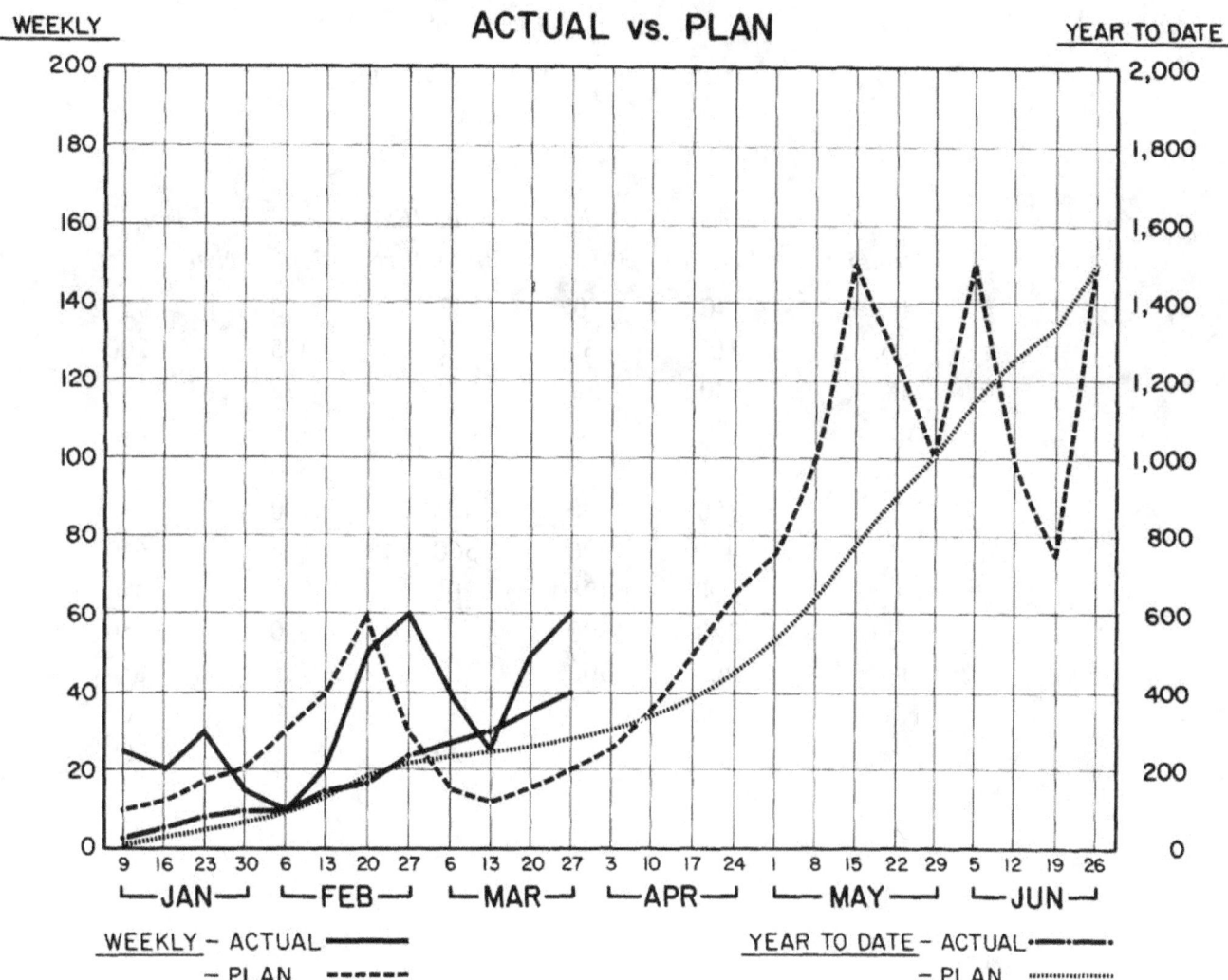

This chart is considered superior to a bar chart. For reference see Bar Charts 17 and 17A.

EXHIBIT FOR LINE CHART 13 AND BAR CHART 18

Alternate Monthly Unit Sales Plans

BOAT DIVISION

UNIT SALES

MONTHLY PLAN VERSUS
ALTERNATIVES

Month	Increase Prices	Reduce Models	Annual Budget	Extra Promotion	Add Ten Distributors
Jan.	40	50	57	65	75
Feb.	100	130	160	175	200
March	30	50	62	75	100
April	100	150	175	190	225
May	300	400	550	600	700
June	350	400	475	700	900
July	400	500	560	575	650
Aug.	100	125	205	225	400
Sept.	220	300	490	510	650
Oct.	400	500	710	725	850
Nov.	200	250	390	400	500
Dec.	50	75	120	150	200

CHART 13

Boat Division
MONTHLY UNIT SALES PLAN vs. ALTERNATIVES

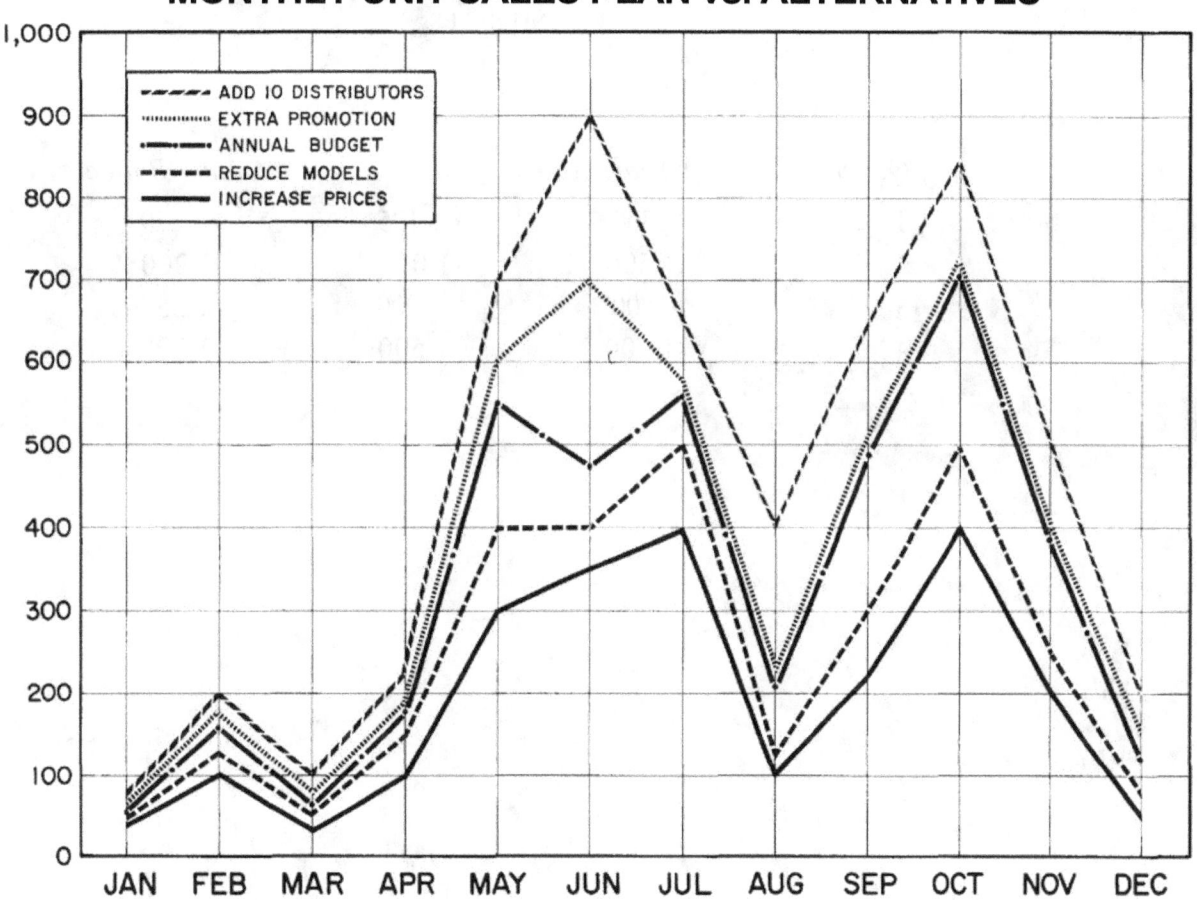

This chart is considered inferior to Bar Chart 18.

EXHIBIT FOR LINE CHART 14 AND BAR CHART 19

Actual Quarterly Unit Sales for Last Two Years and Annual Budget

BOAT DIVISION

UNIT SALES
QUARTERLY

Quarter	Two Years Ago	Last Year	Annual Budget
1	300	125	279
2	1 500	1 000	1 200
3	800	900	1 255
4	1 000	1 500	1 220

CHART 14

Boat Division
QUARTERLY UNIT SALES

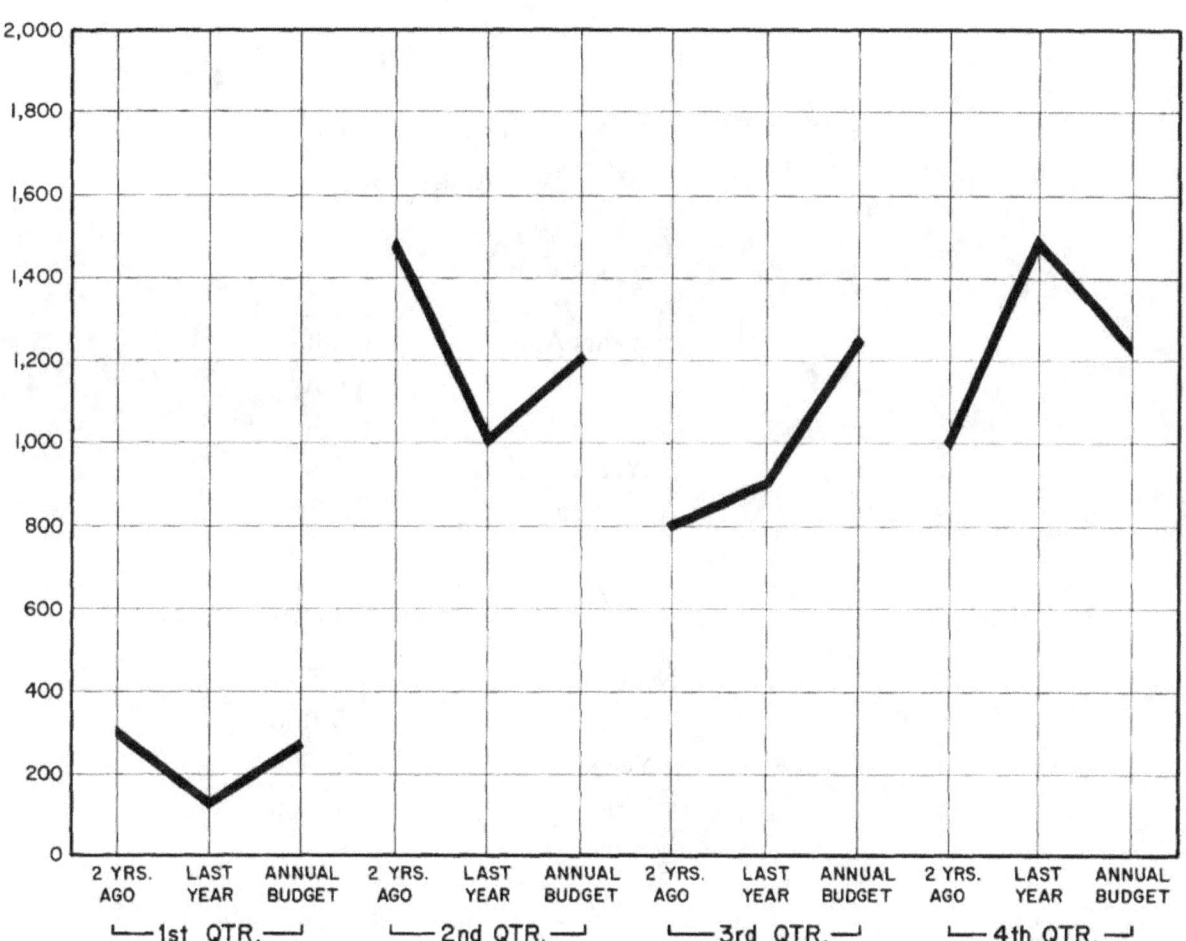

This chart is considered inferior to Bar Chart 19.

71

EXHIBIT FOR LINE CHART 15 AND BAR CHART 20

Actual Unit Sales for Last 5 Years and Annual Budget for Next 5 Years

BOAT DIVISION

UNIT SALES

ANNUAL

	$
5 Years Ago	10 000
4 Years Ago	6 000
3 Years Ago	4 500
2 Years Ago	3 600
Last Year	3 525
Annual Budget	3 954
Next Year	6 500
2 Years	9 000
3 Years	12 000
4 Years	18 000

CHART 15

Boat Division
ANNUAL UNIT SALES

(000)

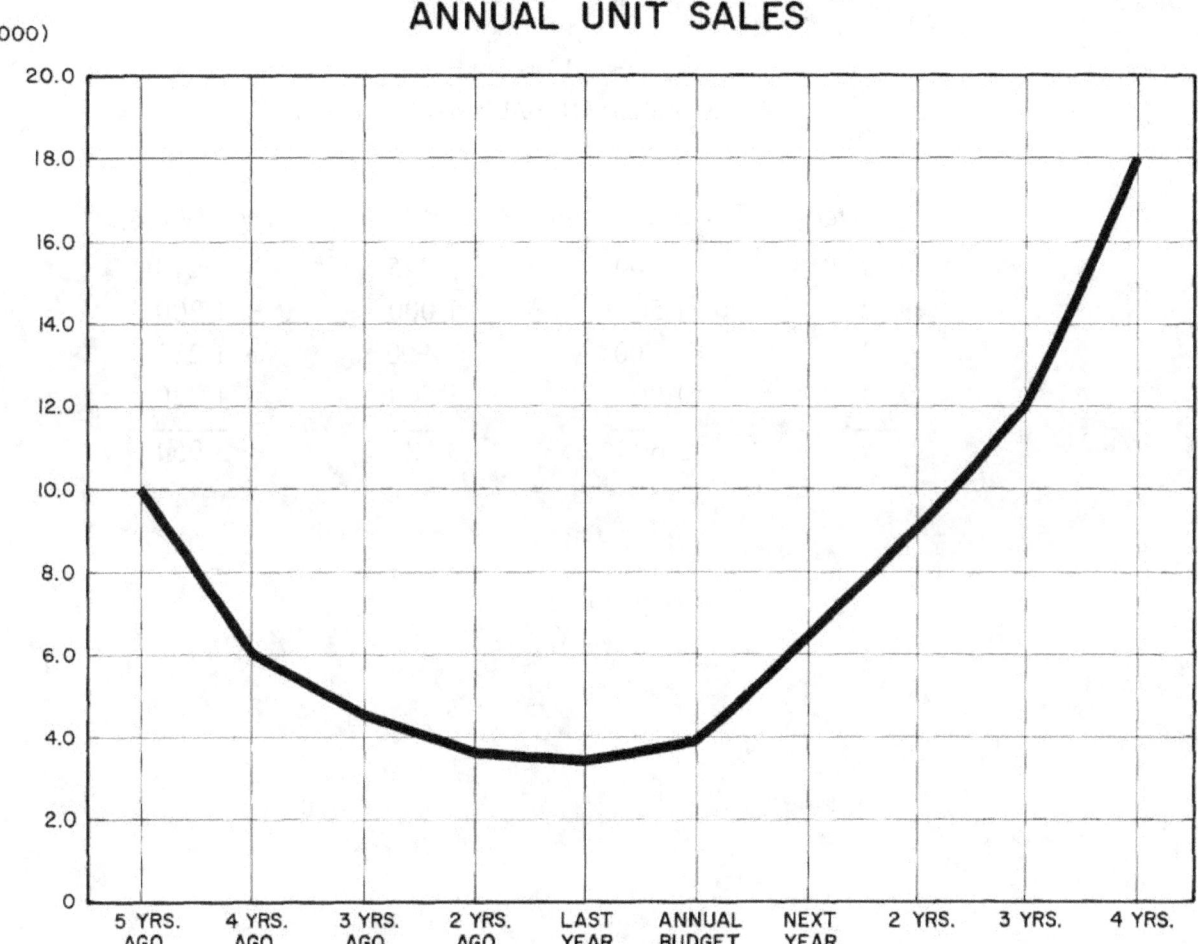

This chart and Bar Chart 20 are both easy to follow and the choice is a matter of individual preference.

EXHIBIT FOR LINE CHART 16 AND BAR CHART 21

BOAT DIVISION

UNIT SALES
COMBINED ANNUAL AND QUARTERLY

Quarter	Two Years Ago	Last Year	Annual Budget
1	300	125	279
2	1 500	1 000	1 200
3	800	900	1 255
4	1 000	1 500	1 220
Y	3 600	3 525	3 954

CHART 16

Boat Division
COMBINED ANNUAL a QUARTERLY UNIT SALES

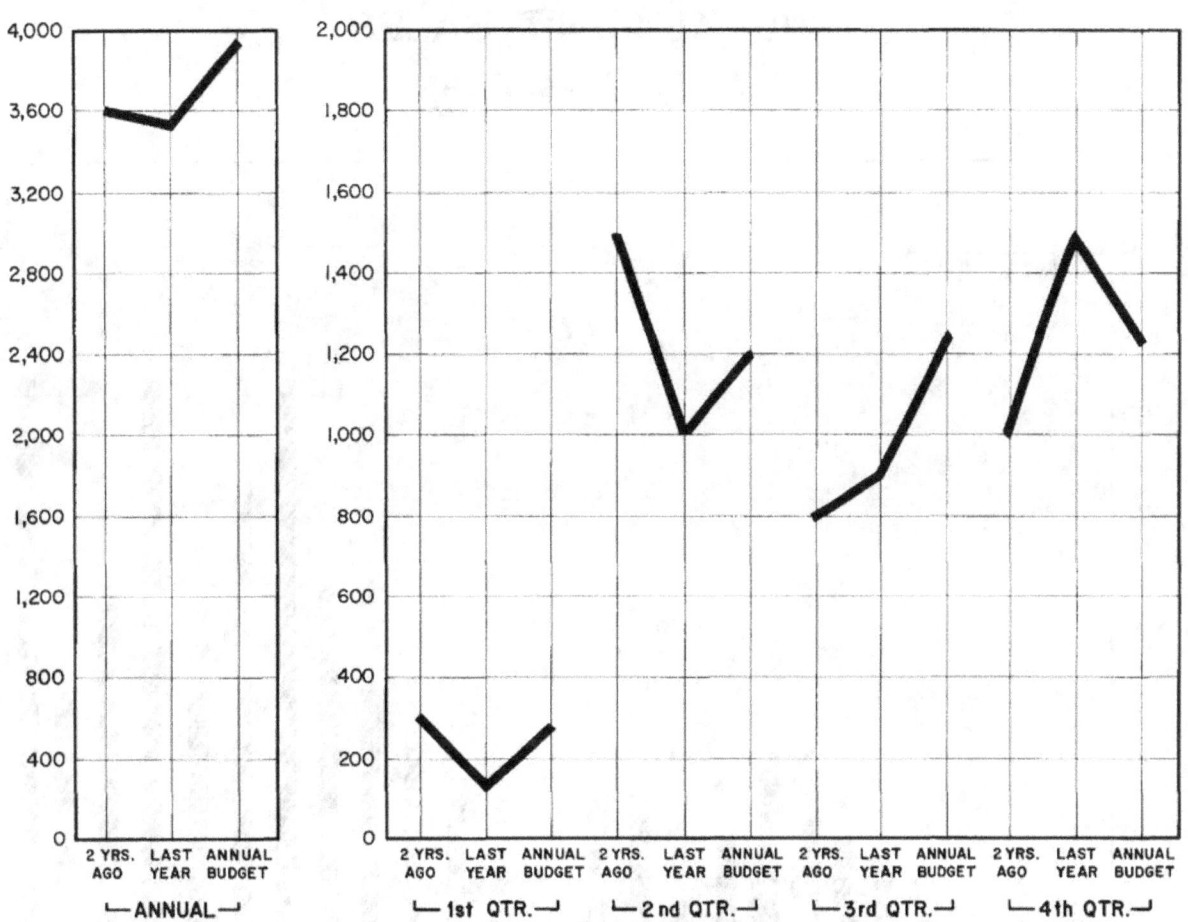

This chart is not recommended. Bar Chart 21 can be more easily interpreted.

CHART 17

Boat Division
WEEKLY UNIT SALES
ACTUAL vs. PLAN

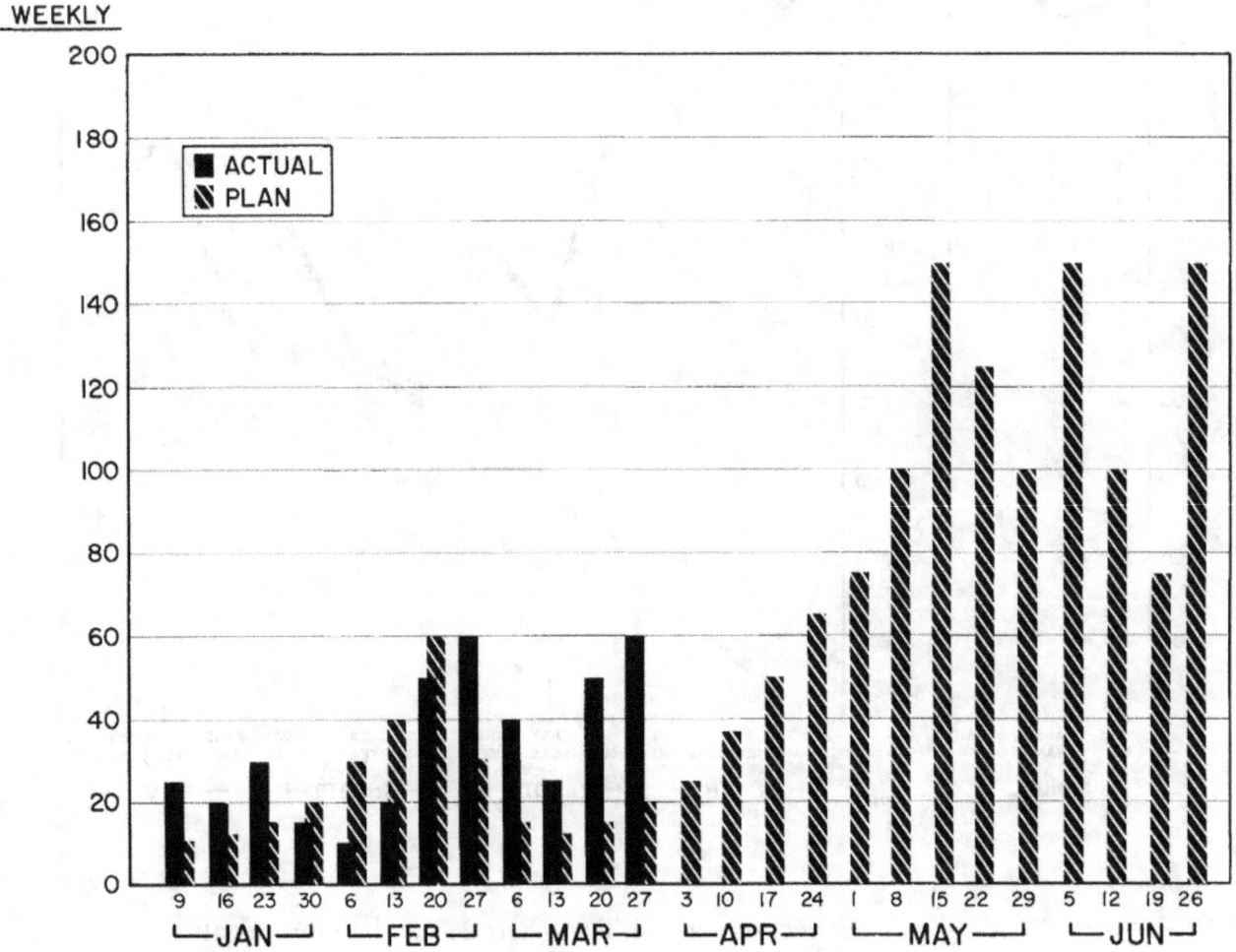

This chart is useful for a restricted amount of data, but it will not accommodate year to date information as easily as Line Chart 12.

Boat Division

YEAR TO DATE

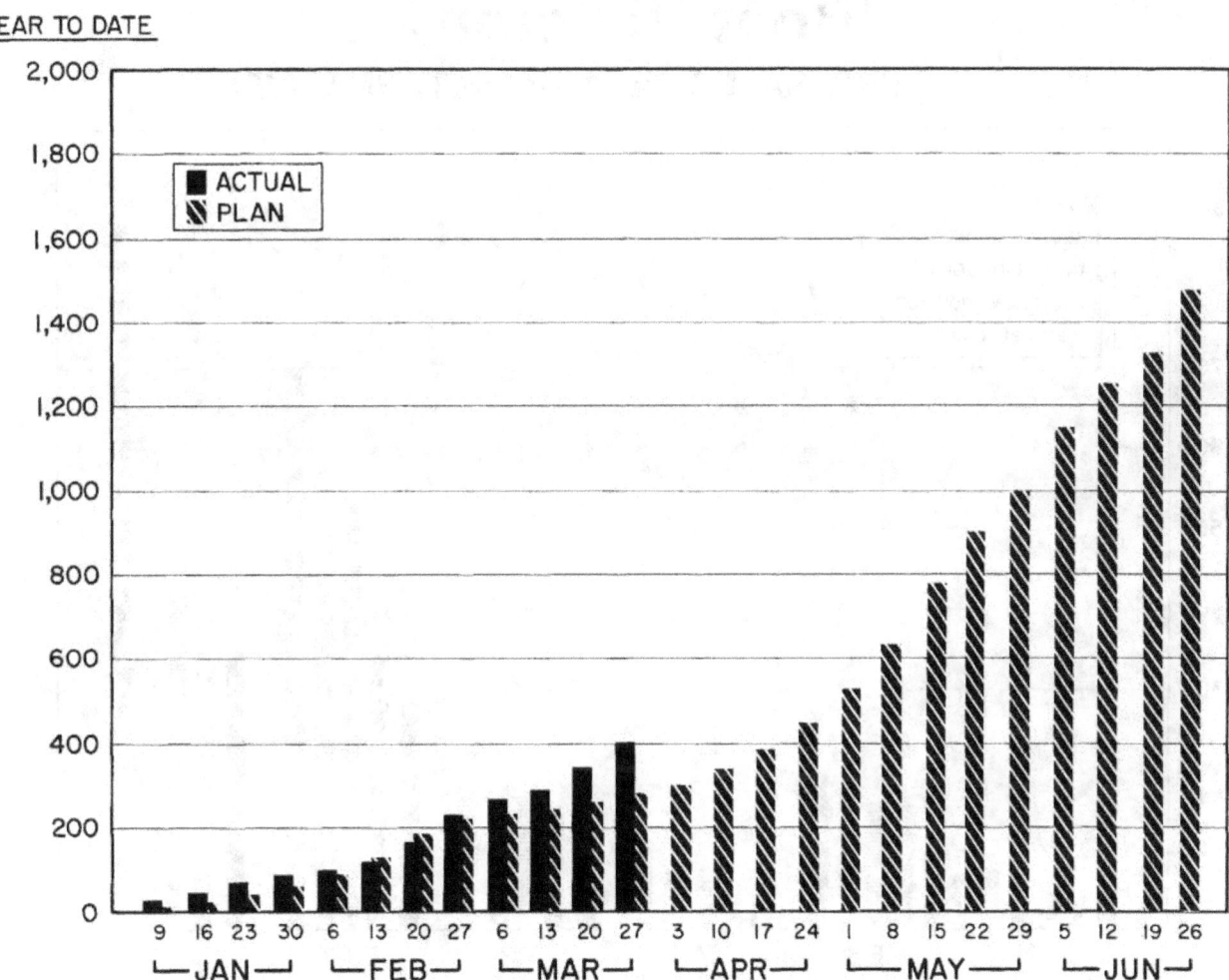

YEAR TO DATE UNIT SALES
ACTUAL vs. PLAN

This chart has the same drawbacks as Bar Chart 17, and is considered inferior to a line chart such as Number 12, if two sets of data are required.

CHART 18

Boat Division

MONTHLY UNIT SALES PLAN vs. ALTERNATIVES

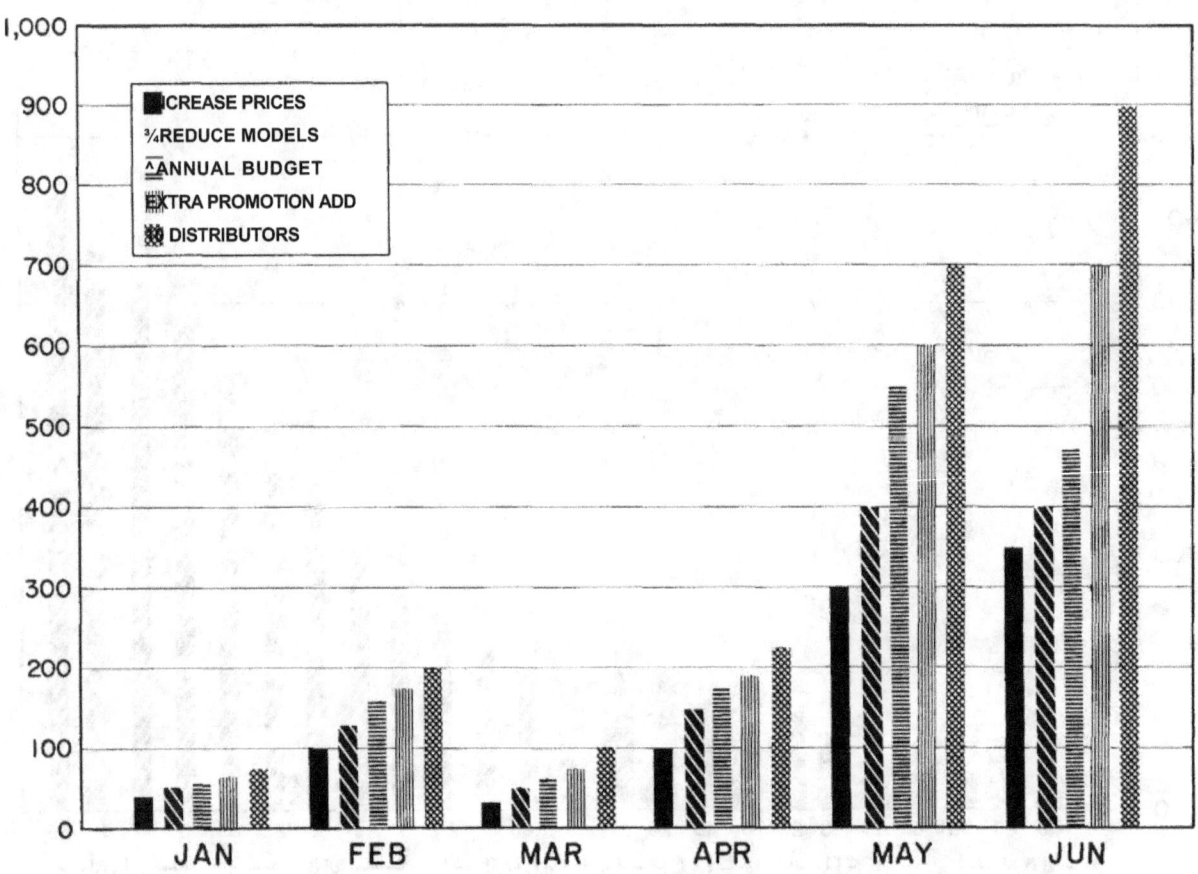

This chart is recommended over Line Chart 13. The improvement in each alternative can be shown as an addition to the original bar, thereby reducing the number of bars required.

Boat Division

CHART 19

QUARTERLY UNIT SALES

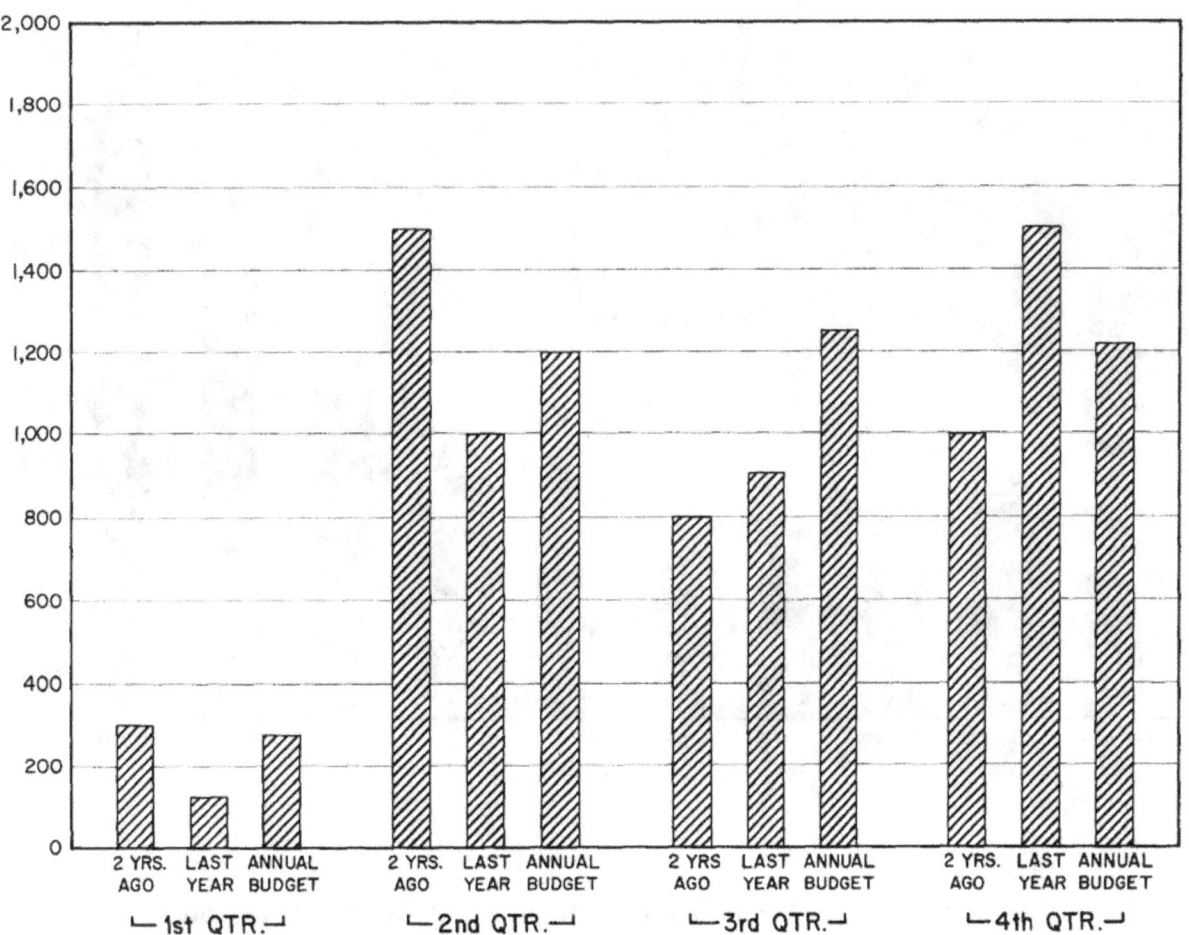

This chart is superior to Line Chart 14.

CHART 20

Boat Division
ANNUAL UNIT SALES
(000)

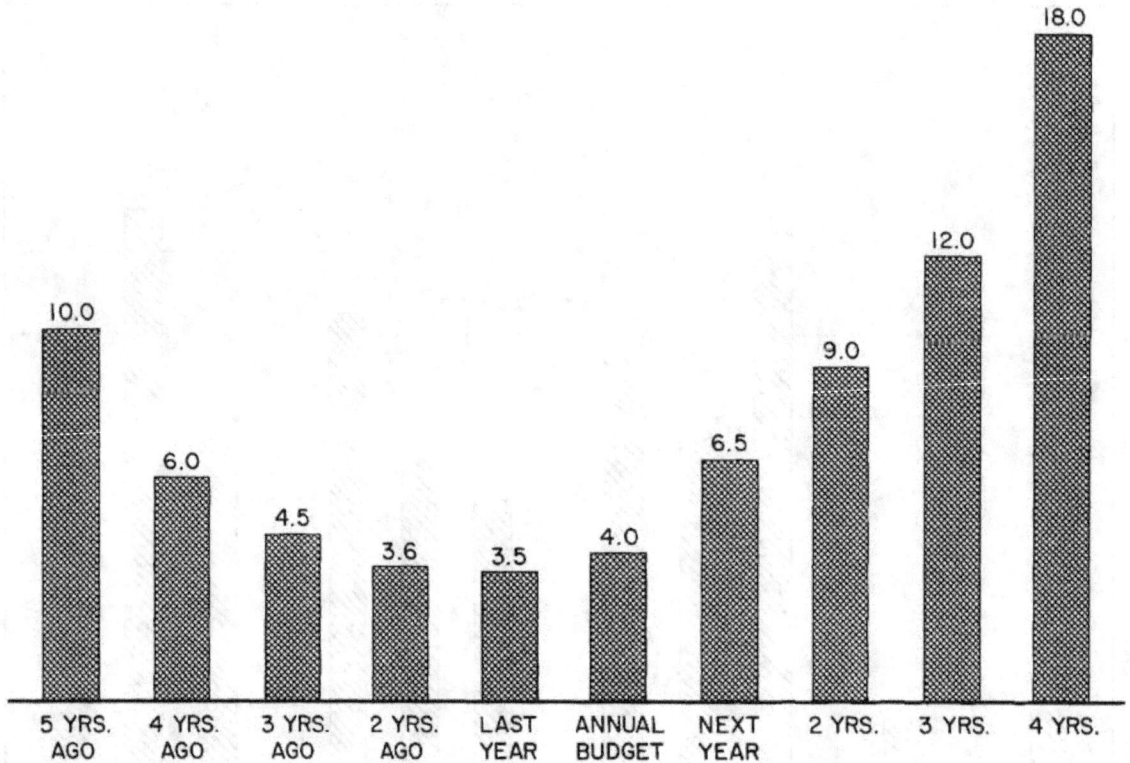

This chart and Line Chart 15 are considered equally informative and the selection is a matter of individual preference.

Boat Division

CHART 21

COMBINED ANNUAL S QUARTERLY UNIT SALES

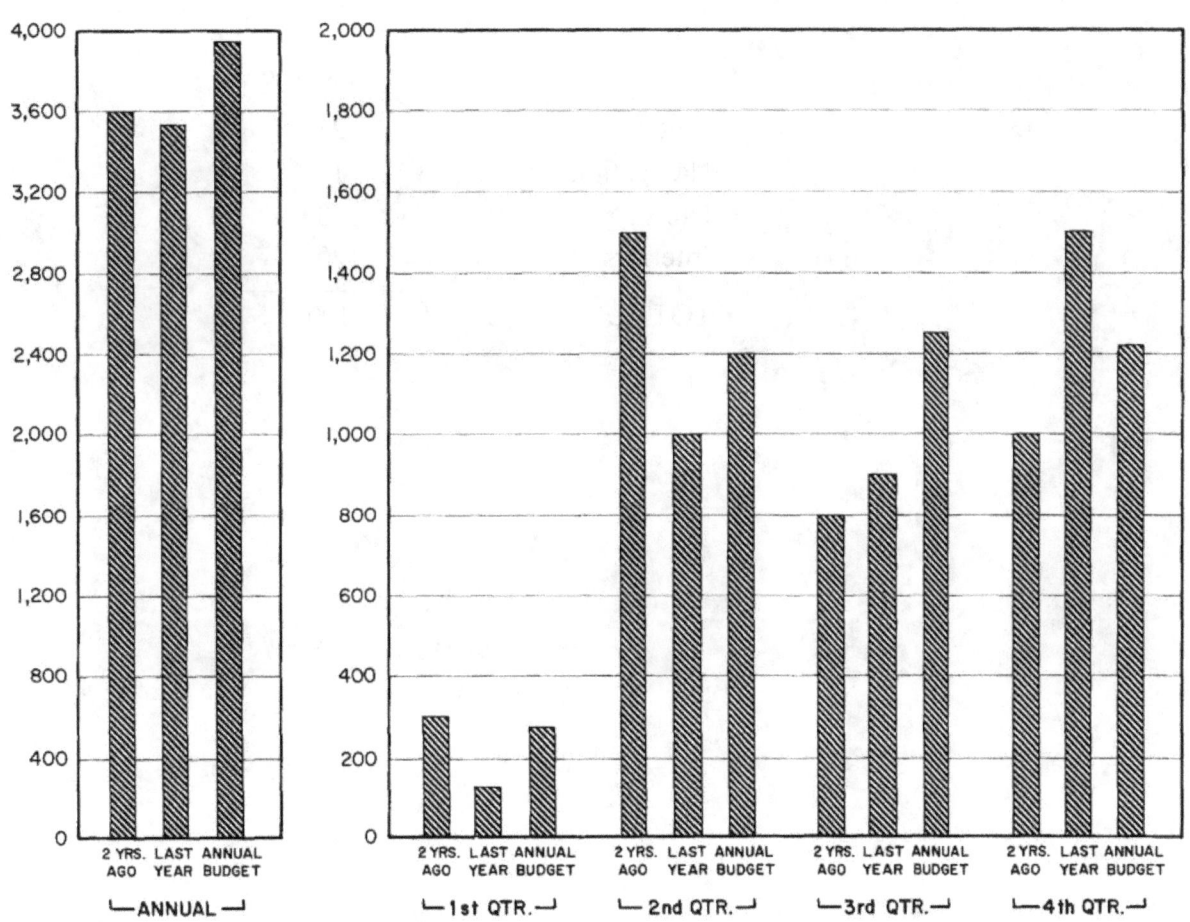

This is highly recommended and is superior to Line Chart 16.

81

EXHIBIT FOR PIE CHART 22

Annual Divisional Sales Budget

BOAT DIVISION

ANNUAL SALES BUDGET

	($ in Millions)
Motors	25
Navigation	15
Hulls	40
Interiors	20
TOTAL	100

CHART 22

Boat Division

ANNUAL SALES BUDGET

($ MILLIONS)

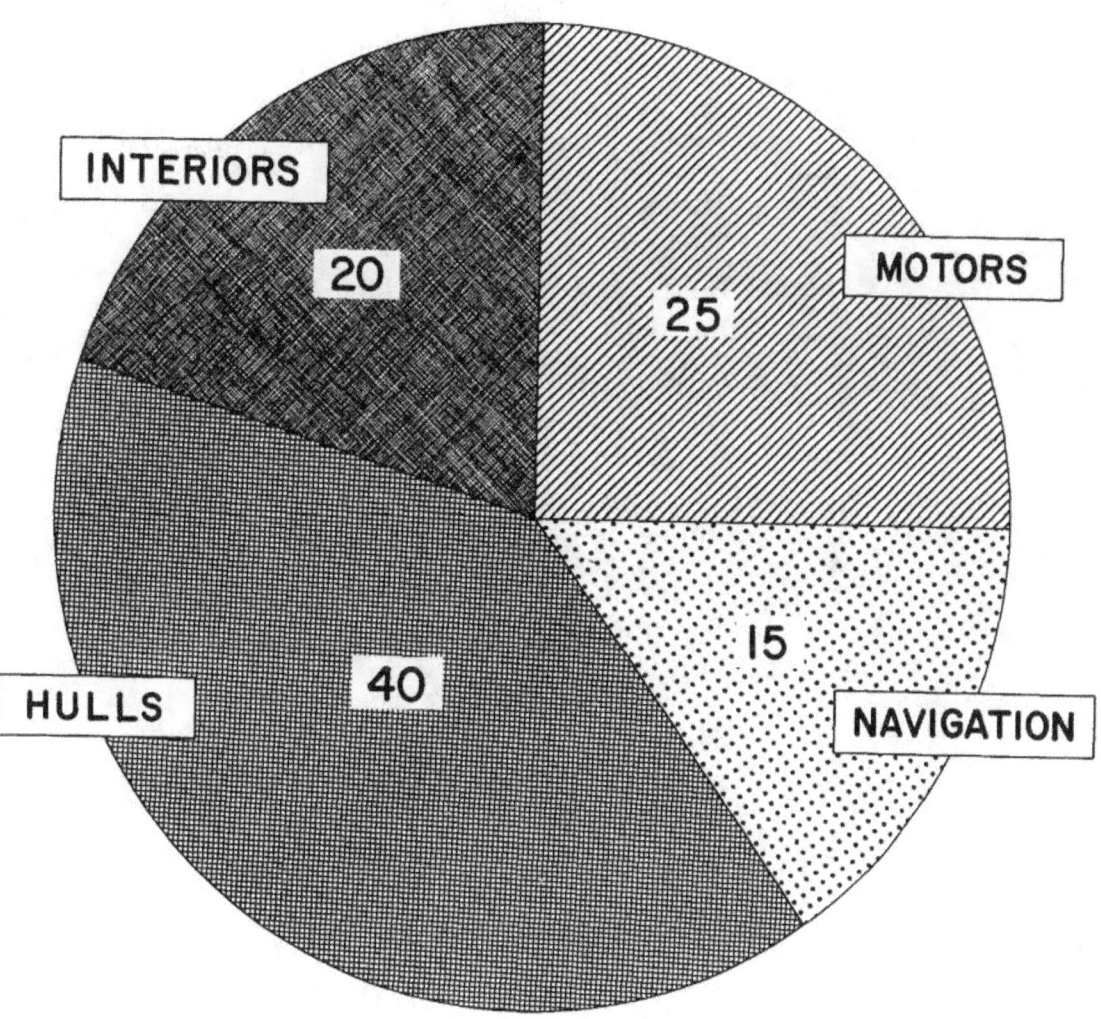

This type of chart, although easy to read, is highly restrictive, and does not permit trend comparisons.

EXHIBIT FOR PIE CHART 23

Annual Divisional Pretax Profit Budget and % to Total Profits

BOAT DIVISION

ANNUAL PRETAX PROFITS

DOLLARS AND % TO TOTAL

($ in Millions)

	Dollars	Percent
Motors	1.5	7.5
Navigation	4.5	22.5
Hulls	4.0	20.0
Interiors	10.0	50.0
TOTAL	20.0	100.0

CHART 23

Boat Division

ANNUAL PRETAX PROFITS & % TO TOTAL
($ MILLIONS)

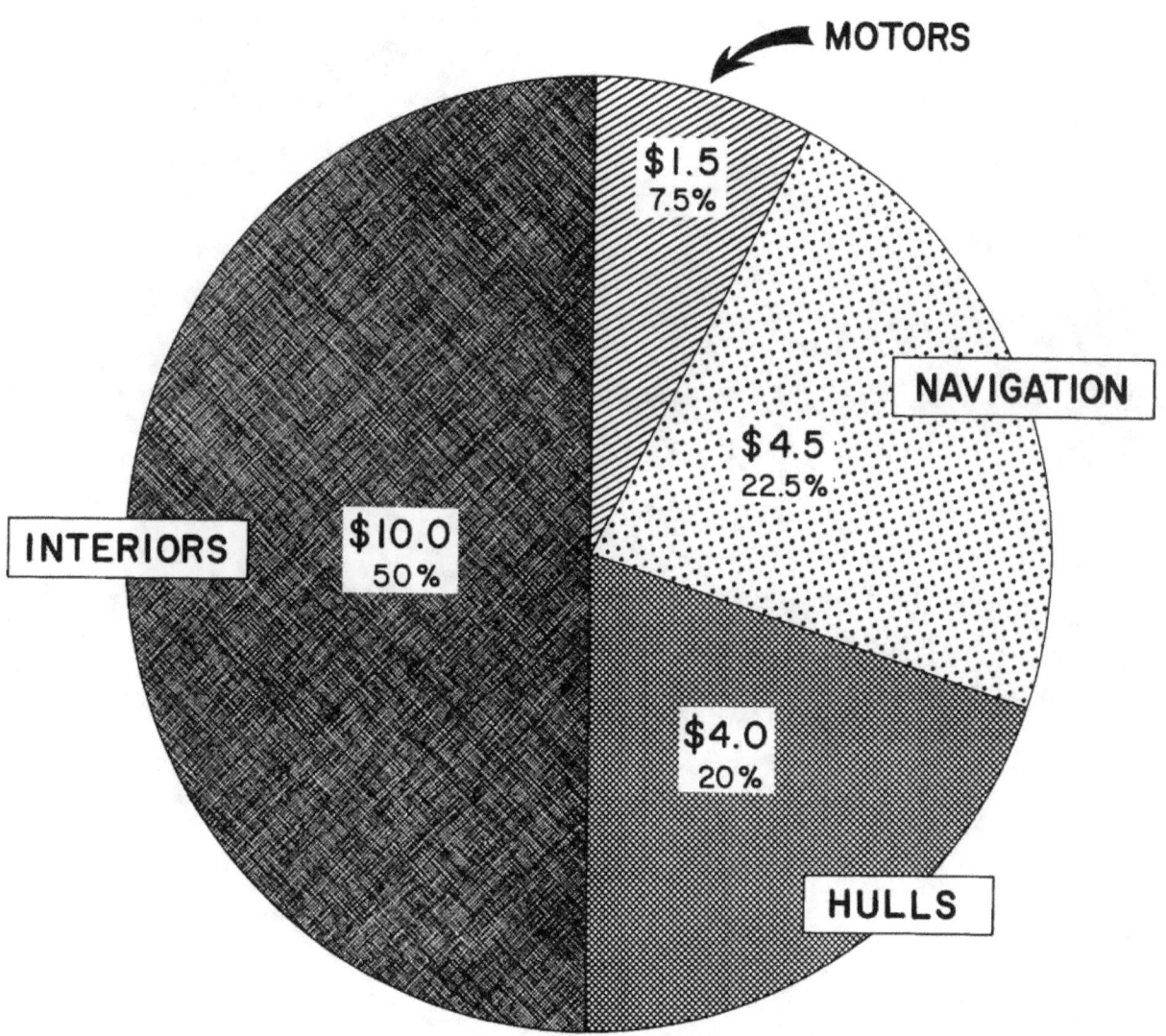

MOTORS

$1.5
7.5%

NAVIGATION

$4.5
22.5%

INTERIORS

$10.0
50%

$4.0
20%

HULLS

This chart is easily interpreted but is not flexible enough for trend evaluation and requires an overlay adaptation if used with a sales chart.

85

FOLLOWING THE SALES TREND

It is necessary in every business to follow sales trends carefully. However, sales statistics tell no story unless they can be compared with prior monthly, quarterly or annual performance; compared with competitor volume; compared with the budget, or compared with the relative performance of other product lines within the company.

Charts can perform the sales comparison job better than any other medium. A table of statistics is difficult to follow and impossible for many individuals to interpret accurately. The interpretive comment necessary to elaborate on several pages of figures can easily lose the reader's interest.

The sales chart can take several forms, depending upon the type of information being presented. The most common sales charts include:

Individual product lines Comparisons
with competitors Comparisons with
other product lines

Individual Product Lines

If a single product is involved, the annual and quarterly volume can be shown on one chart using bars. This technique is illustrated on Chart 24, which shows annual and quarterly sales for the Motor Division of The Francis Company. The left section of the chart has bars depicting each year for the past several years, the current year, and provision for the next two years.

Immediately to the right of the annual bars are a series of bars divided by the four quarters of the year. The first group of bars represents the first quarter and shows the same years selected for the annual information. The second set of bars is for the second quarter of each year; the next group for the third quarter, followed by the fourth quarter of each year.

This presentation tells the management several important facts:

1. Are annual sales going up or down or remaining constant?
2. Is the quarterly trend improving each year, getting worse, or becoming stagnant?
3. Is any one quarter improving or worsening, compared with the other quarters?
4. Is one quarter bearing the brunt of the year's volume?
5. Is there a shift in income from one quarter to another?

The answers to these questions will largely determine executive action with respect to:

Sales policy
Advertising and Promotion
Manufacturing
Purchasing
Distribution

It is imperative that charts of this type be kept up to date. The top corporate management should review the sales performance with the divisional management on a regular basis, preferably once a month, or even weekly if short term sales fluctuations are volatile.

By a careful scrutiny of sales trends an alert management will be in a position to take quick and effective action. Charts will reveal the downturns and accurately reflect the seriousness of volume changes. Charts in this manner become a direct aid to managing the business and improving profits. Charts should compare actual results with budgets. This actual versus budget technique is illustrated in Chapter 8, dealing with the Control of Costs.

The sales statistics used on the charts may be obtained from several sources. Usually the sales or marketing department, the economist and the accounting department have data on a weekly, monthly, quarterly and annual basis.

The exact source of these statistics must be determined, prior to beginning a chart program. It must be understood that the information emanating from a particular source will be furnished on a regular basis and in a consistent manner. It is very important that when the basic concept of an operation changes the figures being charted be re-classified to avoid distortion and misinterpretation. It must also be appreciated, however, that different sources can and should be tapped depending upon the type of information required and the use of the charts. For example, while the accounting department will probably have gross and net sales by product lines, the sales department may have finer product breakdowns by high, medium and low end merchandise, by distributor, by market area, by model and so on. It is possible that all of these figures come from the accounting department or tabulating section; but the particular refinements and interpretation should be the responsibility of the sales or marketing group.

When the proper information has been obtained and charted, the cycle is two-thirds completed. Prior to hanging the charts or making any widespread distribution, they should be reviewed with the sales management, in addition to the responsible financial people. A sound chart program can become useless if there is a lack of understanding, or the operating executive has no opportunity to prepare himself for possible questions from the top executive management. It is entirely possible that the original review may indicate that information has been improperly assembled and the true picture distorted. It is easier to redo the chart than to explain away the wrong information. This is an elementary suggestion, but one which is frequently ignored, with disastrous results.

THE FRANCIS COMPANY
MOTOR DIVISION

FACTORY DOLLAR SALES
ANNUALLY BY QUARTERS

Quarters

	First	Second	Third	Fourth	Total Year
4 Years Ago	$ 9 000	$10 100	$15 400	$17 000	$51 500
3 Years Ago	12 000	10 400	20 300	14 500	57 200
2 Years Ago	8 700	5 500	17 400	17 600	49 200
Last Year	8 000	8 500	15 800	13 700	46 000
This Year	7 800	4 200	8 900	13 300	34 200
Next Year	10 000	12 000	18 000	12 000	52 000
Data for Chart	24	24	24	24	24

Comments

The sales chart indicates a steady deterioration in annual volume, but a much slower loss of fourth quarter revenue.

It is apparent that the sales department is quite optimistic about next year's potential. An upturn of these dimensions, following a continuous downward trend over a three-year period, should be questioned by the management. The projected recoveries in each of the first three quarters are particularly suspect. Inquiry should be made with respect to whether the expected increases result from new customers, increased prices, more extensive coverage, additional distributors, a new product line, etc.

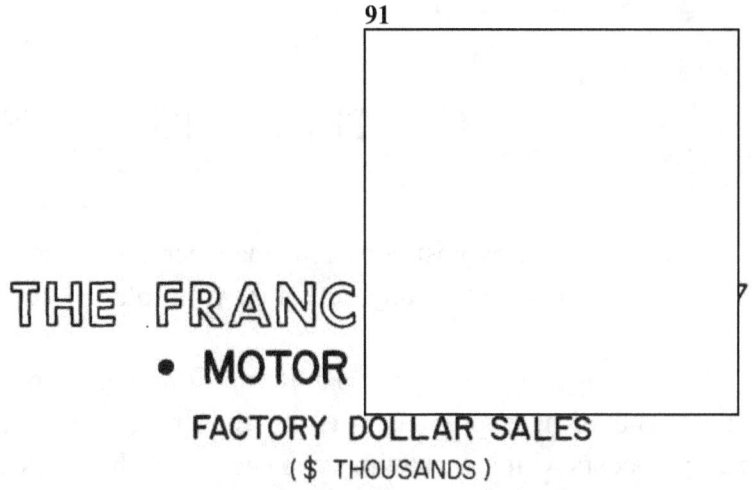

THE FRANC...

• MOTOR

FACTORY DOLLAR SALES

($ THOUSANDS)

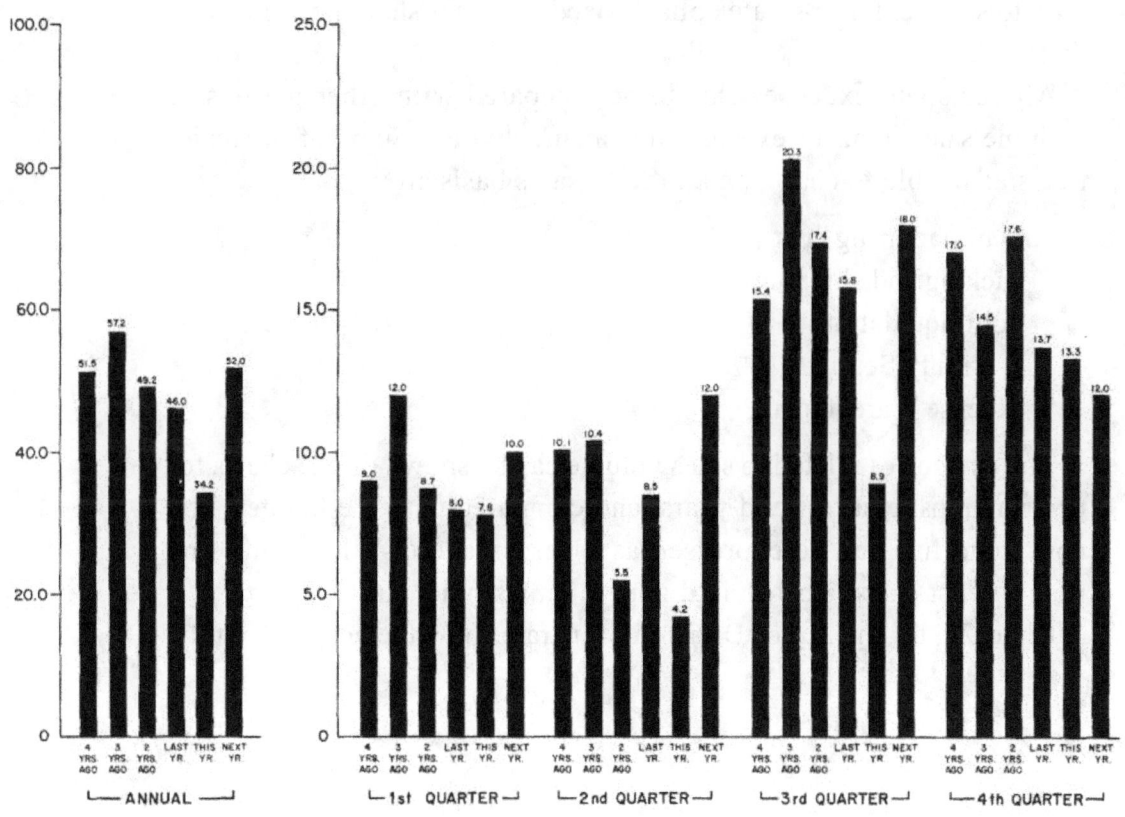

CHART
24

8

CONTROLLING COSTS

Successful businesses are run by cost-conscious managements. Charts will help control costs by highlighting any departure from planned expenditures.

Charts should deal with those major cost items which are controllable. The costs should be expressed in terms appropriate to their control. For example, costs which vary with sales should be shown as a ratio to sales and in absolute dollars; fixed expenses should be plotted in dollars.

All costs and expenses should be compared with other periods or with the same items of expense in similar activities. Some of the major items adaptable to charts on a ratio to sales basis are:

    Manufacturing cost
    Packing and shipping
    Tool liquidation
    Warranty Selling
    expense Warehousing

The categories related to sales volume can be shown on the charts for prior months, quarters and years, and compared with the budget. The cost trend line can be expressed as a percentage of sales. Only one item of cost or expense should appear on a single chart.

Chart 25, for the Motor Division, illustrates how the actual monthly manufacturing cost ratio to sales, for the current year, compares with the budget. The figures at the top of the bar represent the dollar amounts, in thousands. The lines in the upper section of the chart indicate the related manufacturing cost ratios to sales.

Chart 26, for the Motor Division, shows how this same monthly information, on the manufacturing dollar cost, can be plotted on a line chart. The ratio to sales appears at the bottom of the chart.

The most useful of these two types of presentation is a matter of individual preference. The author would recommend Chart 25; it clearly demonstrates the seriousness of any unfavorable cost trend and properly relates the dollar costs to sales volume. Either type of chart will focus management attention on a serious problem, not only of increasing costs, but the need for additional volume in order to absorb overhead. The approach adopted for manufacturing cost would also apply to the other items, namely packing and shipping, tool liquidation, warranty, selling expense, warehousing and similar costs and expenses.

It would, of course, be expected that in a fully developed chart program a monthly and quarterly summary of actual performance versus budget would be prepared, using either bar charts or line charts. In addition, for purposes of closer control at the lower management levels, it would be desirable to have charts indicating the basic factors affecting these manufacturing costs, such as material, labor and overhead.

The following schedule provides the statistical information for Charts 25 and 26.

EXHIBIT FOR CHARTS 25 and 26

THE FRANCIS COMPANY
MOTOR DIVISION

Sales and Manufacturing Costs
and Percent to Sales
This Year by Months
(Actual vs. Budget)

	ACTUAL			BUDGET		
	Sales	Mfg. Cost	% to Sales	Sales	Mfg. Cost	% to Sales
January	$ 2 900	$ 2 100	73	$ 2 900	$ 2 000	70
February	2 700	2 000	73	3 400	2 300	68
March	2 200	1 500	66	3 400	2 200	65
April	1 200	650	54	3 100	2 100	67
May	1 100	600	55	3 200	2 200	68
June	1 900	1 100	58	4 600	2 900	63
July	2 100	1 400	66	3 500	2 400	69
August	1 700	1 050	62	4 200	2 500	59
September	5 100	3 100	60	6 800	3 900	57
October	5 700	3 500	62	5 600	3 300	59
November	4 900	3 200	66	5 500	3 300	60
December	2 700	2 100	76	3 400	2 200	65
Year	$34 200	$22 300	65	$49 600	$31 300	63
Data for Charts		25&26	25 & 26		25&26	25 & 26

94

CHART 25

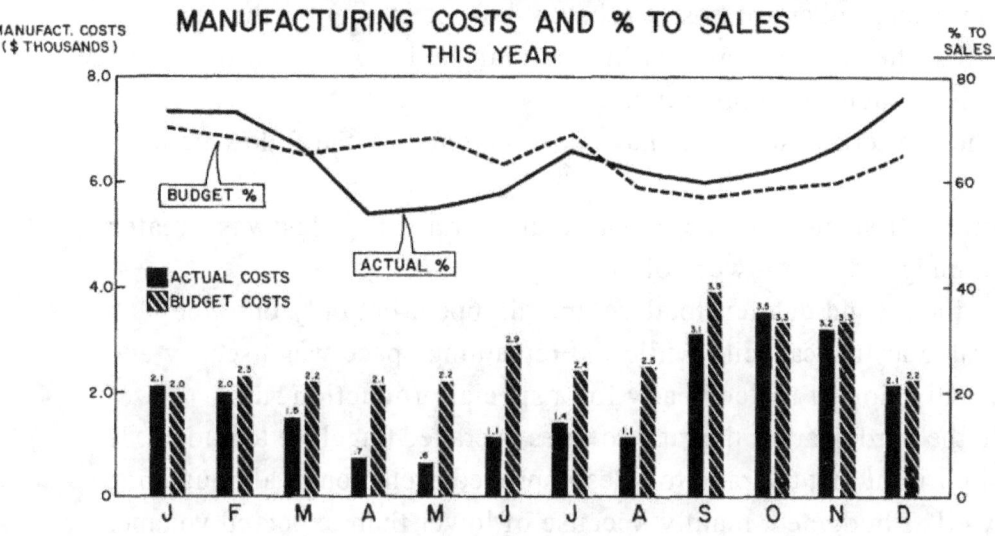

THE FRANCIS COMPANY
• MOTOR DIVISION •
MANUFACTURING COSTS AND % TO SALES
THIS YEAR

MANUFACT. COSTS
($ THOUSANDS)

% TO
SALES

BUDGET %

ACTUAL %

■ ACTUAL COSTS
▨ BUDGET COSTS

J F M A M J J A S O N D

CHART 26

MANUFACT. COSTS
($ THOUSANDS)

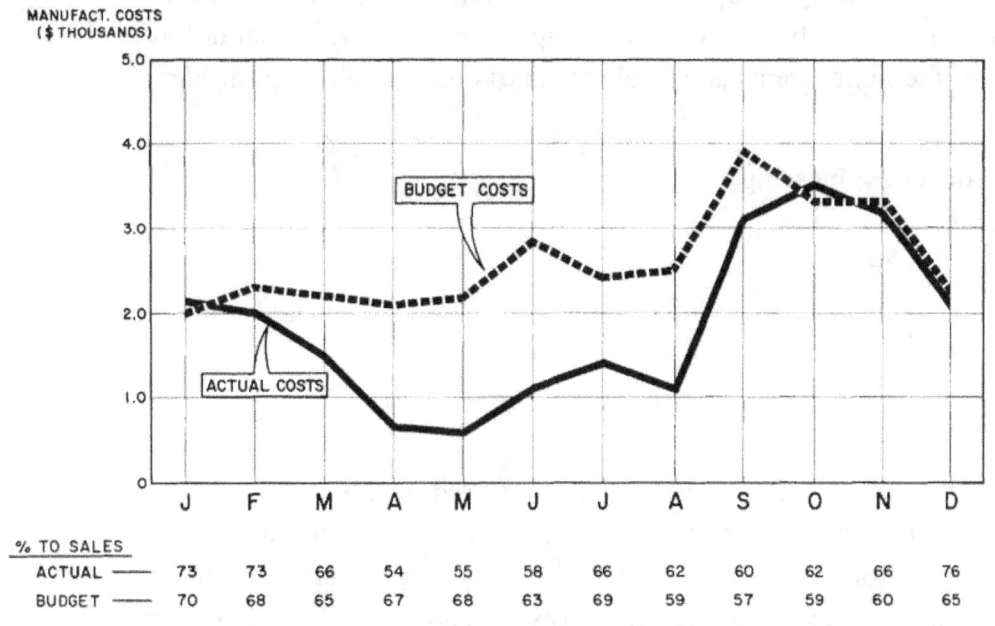

BUDGET COSTS

ACTUAL COSTS

J F M A M J J A S O N D

% TO SALES												
ACTUAL ——	73	73	66	54	55	58	66	62	60	62	66	76
BUDGET ——	70	68	65	67	68	63	69	59	57	59	60	65

Comments

Chart 25 tells a significant story with its ratio to sales message: while actual dollars of cost are below budget in four of the last five months, the ratio to sales is higher than budget. This is the trend which management must reverse.

The quarterly results may have been affected by the following conditions:

In the first quarter, the manufacturing ratio to sales was greater than budget due to lower volume.

In the second quarter, total volume dropped, but only one line was operated at full capacity while the remaining space was used by another division of the company for a special production run.

In the third quarter, the ratio to sales averaged out close to budget. It is significant that the ratio to sales improved each month, although not as well as budgeted, mainly because of lower than expected volume.

In the fourth quarter the manufacturing cost ratio to sales exceeded budget by a wide margin, as a result of start-up costs on a new model, frequent engineering changes and a substantial amount of down time.

This type of analysis should accompany each chart presentation. Some of the major items adaptable to charts on a fixed amount basis are:

> Product engineering
> Plant and equipment
> Purchasing
> Advertising
> Financial
> Legal
> Executive

Relatively stable items ot expense, not geared to sales, can be illustrated by lines or bars which represent dollars. The variations in the lines or bars for past, present and future periods can quickly point to problem areas. Each chart should be restricted to one type of cost or expense. This type of presentation is shown on Chart 27, for advertising expense. It compares quarterly dollar spending for last year and this year with the budget for this year. The percentages at the bottom of the chart indicate the advertising expense ratio to sales.

It is extremely important to bring both the dollar amounts *and* the advertising expense ratios to the attention of management. In a situation such as illustrated by the Motor Division, it may be necessary to greatly increase the advertising authorization in order to recoup a lost market position. Under the circumstances, advertising expenses cannot be evaluated strictly on a sales ratio basis; instead they must be considered in the light of expected volume increases, new customers to be reached, additional territories to be covered, etc.

A company will find it difficult to solve a sales volume problem by curtailing advertising expenditures. This point must be emphasized when presenting the chart information. This is the primary reason for having the bars reflect advertising dollars instead of the advertising ratio to sales; the dollars are much more important. *The control must be exercised by making certain that adequate value is being realized for each dollar being spent.* Chart 27 illustrates how both dollar and ratio to sales information for advertising, or other types' of expenses, can be presented.

Expense comparisons can be used to establish incentives based on the attainment of cost reduction goals. The goals should be determined at the beginning of the year, and then compared on a chart with the actual monthly, quarterly and year to date performance. This type of presentation will add to the effectiveness of meeting goal standards and will do much to lower costs and improve profits. For example, it often becomes obvious that outside professional services are getting out of hand. Minimum allowances for these services should be established at the top level each year and the various departments judged monthly or quarterly on their expenditures. If this type of chart is acceptable for advertising expenses, it should also be used to portray similar items such as product engineering, plant and equipment, purchasing, financial, legal, executive, etc.

EXHIBIT FOR CHART 27

THE FRANCIS COMPANY
MOTOR DIVISION

Sales, Advertising Expenses and Percent to Sales
Last Year, This Year and Budget
By Quarters

	Quarters				Full Year	Data For Chart	Last
	First	*Second*	*Third*	*Fourth*			
Year							
Sales	$8 000	$ 8 500	$15 800	$13 700	$46 000		
Advertising Exp.	$ 425	$ 325	$ 625	$ 825	$ 2 200	27	
% to Sales	5	4	4		6	5	27
This Year							
Sales	$7 800	$ 4 200	$ 8 900	$13 300	$34 200		
Advertising Exp.	$ 575	$ 775	$ 950	$ 1 250	$ 3 550	27	
% to Sales	7	18	11		9	10	27
Budget This Year							
Sales	$9 700	$10 900	$14 500	$14 500	$49 600		
Advertising Exp.	$ 500	$ 600	$ 800	$ 900	$ 2 800	27	
% to Sales	5	6	6	6		6	27

CHART 27

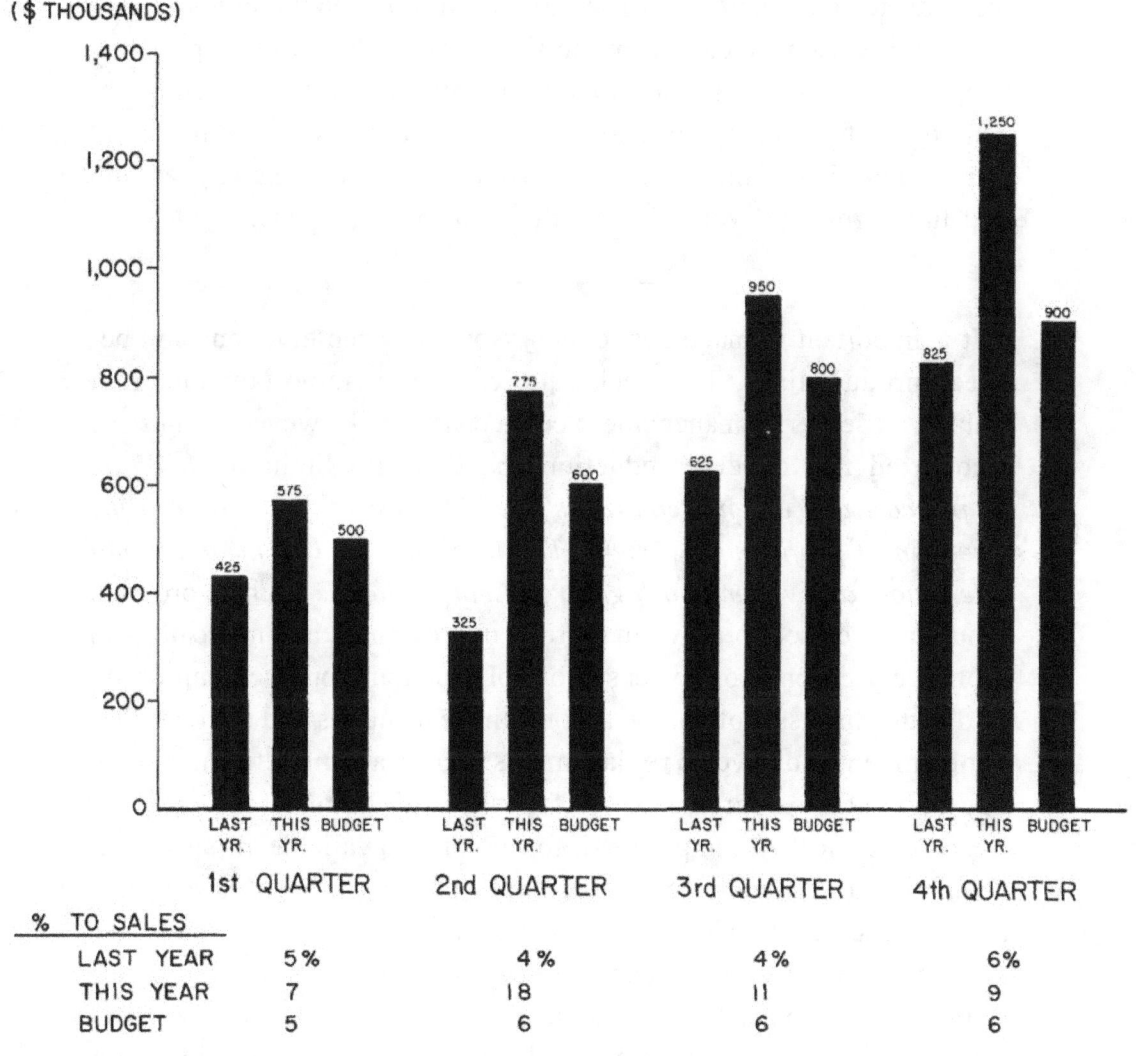

THE FRANCIS COMPANY
• MOTOR DIVISION •
QUARTERLY ADVERTISING EXPENSE

($ THOUSANDS)

% TO SALES			
LAST YEAR	5%	4%	4%	6%
THIS YEAR	7	18	11	9
BUDGET	5	6	6	6

Comments

It became obvious to the management, at the time this year's budget was prepared, that continued sales slippage dictated a heavier dollar advertising outlay. However, with the expectation for greater volume, the budgeted advertising expense ratio to sales moved up only slightly.

When it became apparent, in the first quarter, that sales were below budget, a decision was made to substantially increase advertising expenditures. This was too late to help second quarter volume, but it did start an upswing in the third and fourth quarters, with the expectation that future revenue would justify the additional expense.

———————————————

It is important to make cost comparisons between divisions and between product lines. This technique can be an important factor in making all levels of management cost conscious. However, it must be recognized that expense reductions have severe limitations. *While proper cost and expense control is vital, it goes only part way in the direction of profit improvement. The final answer lies in additional sales effort and volume on high gross margin items.* A chart program should not be used to prove that profit improvement automatically and exclusively depends on expense control. Such an approach can easily lead to the dismissal of young, second-line executives and the retention of older men who have no replacements upon reaching retirement age. Too often chart programs go too far in this direction.

It is seldom that competitor information is available in sufficient detail to chart the more important elements of cost. For this reason it may be necessary to adapt your expense classifications to those of your competitors whenever another company does release this type of information and you wish to make such a comparison. Generally, however, published competitor data is sketchy and cannot be relied upon to be comparable. Rather than attempt competitor cost comparisons it is recommended that this phase of the chart program confine itself to sales, profits, assets, profit per cent to sales and return on assets and/or net worth.

9

EVALUATING PROFITS

Business survival is dependent upon satisfactory profits. However, it is necessary to realize that earnings must be satisfactory both in absolute dollars and in relation to investment. A chart quickly pinpoints unfavorable profit trends by products, by divisions, and for the total company.

Charts can put profit in the proper perspective. This is not always so with statistics; the reader can be easily misled by a statistical interpretation. Profits should be expressed in three ways in order that the management fully understands the significance of the story the chart has to tell:

1. In absolute dollars.
2. As a percent to sales.
3. As a percent return on assets.

Profits for a division should be compared with those of another division and with the company's leading competitor. Each division should compare its current profits with the results of the past five years and with a forecast of the next five years. The current picture should be expressed by months, quarters, year to date and the full year. The profit chart should be updated monthly and the most recent forecast should be plotted, and compared with the annual budget for the period.

When divisional profits have been charted and analyzed, additional

101

charts should show profits for each of the major product lines within the division. These charts will reveal whether one or two products are supporting the other lines. Oftentimes this type of analysis can lead to the dropping of unsatisfactory products, to the benefit of the division and the company. Charts will provide a clearer understanding of profit comparisons than any other means of presentation.

Charts permit the management to evaluate the changes which have occurred between actual performance and the projections. This should lead to requests for written explanations of why earnings are not on target, are not better than in prior periods, or do not exceed a competitor's performance.

If the top executive properly uses the charts, a continuous profit review and evaluation program can be undertaken which will benefit all levels of management.

Charts can be used to observe profits under a variety of policy alternatives. For example, a trend line can indicate the level of profits over the past five years and compare them with the most recent forecast for the next five years. The projected profit line can then be recast to indicate the effect of:

1. Price changes.
2. Volume fluctuations.
3. Cost reductions.
4. Changes in distribution methods.
5. Increasing advertising, promotion and sales costs.
6. Extending territorial coverage.
7. Product redesign.
8. Introducing new models.
9. Building a new plant.
10. Acquiring a competitor company.

The results of any management plan can be quickly plotted on the profit chart and compared with the results of doing business under existing conditions. A chart is an invaluable management tool when it can visually demonstrate the level of profits to be expected from any of several courses of action.

The following charts illustrate the complete grasp the management has of the profit situation when it reviews earnings from the standpoint of:

A. The last five years versus the next five years, expressed in dollars.

B. The 10-year period shown as a ratio to sales.

C. The 10 years expressed as a return on assets.

D. Last year, this year and next year, by quarters. This chart shows only dollars, but the ratio charts also can be prepared.

E. Actual performance over the last five years compared with its major competitor. This chart shows both the pretax dollar and return on asset comparisons. It emphasizes that while the Motor Division has been slipping, its number one competitor has been utilizing its assets much more effectively. In a comparison of this kind it is suggested that the competitor's balance sheet be carefully analyzed for unusual items. For ex ample, if in this case it was found that the other company had excess cash, its lead over the Motor Division, on an adjusted basis, would be even greater. In such circumstances both operating units should reflect the same cash base, in order to produce a meaningful comparison.

The following schedule contains the statistics for a 10-year review of profits expressed in dollars, the 10-year story of the profit percent to sales, and the return on assets. This information covers charts 28, 29 and 30.

EXHIBIT FOR CHARTS 28, 29 and 30

THE FRANCIS COMPANY
MOTOR DIVISION

Pretax Profits, % to Sales
and % Return on Assets
10-Year Review

	Sales	Pretax Profits	% to Sales	% Return on Assets
4 Years Ago	$ 51 500	$ 7 700	15	32
3 Years Ago	57 200	6 900	12	24
2 Years Ago	49 200	4 900	10	19
Last Year	46 000	4 100	9	17
This Year	34 200	1 700	5	9
Next Year	52 000	1 600	3	7
2 Years	60 000	3 600	6	15
3 Years	70 000	5 600	8	21
4 Years	85 000	10 200	12	32
5 Years	110 000	18 700	17	48
Data for Charts		28	29	30

Comments

This 10-year profit review, expressed in both absolute dollars and ratios, is invaluable. It is readily apparent that the charts present a better grasp of the situation than do the statistics.

These charts reveal that the Motor Division was prosperous in the past. It also indicates some pessimism for another year. The remarkable upsurge predicted for the later years must be examined in the light of necessary expenditures for facilities, equipment, manpower, new types of materials, etc. In any projection of this sort the divisional

CHART 28

THE FRANCIS COMPANY
• MOTOR DIVISION •
PRETAX PROFIT
($ THOUSANDS)

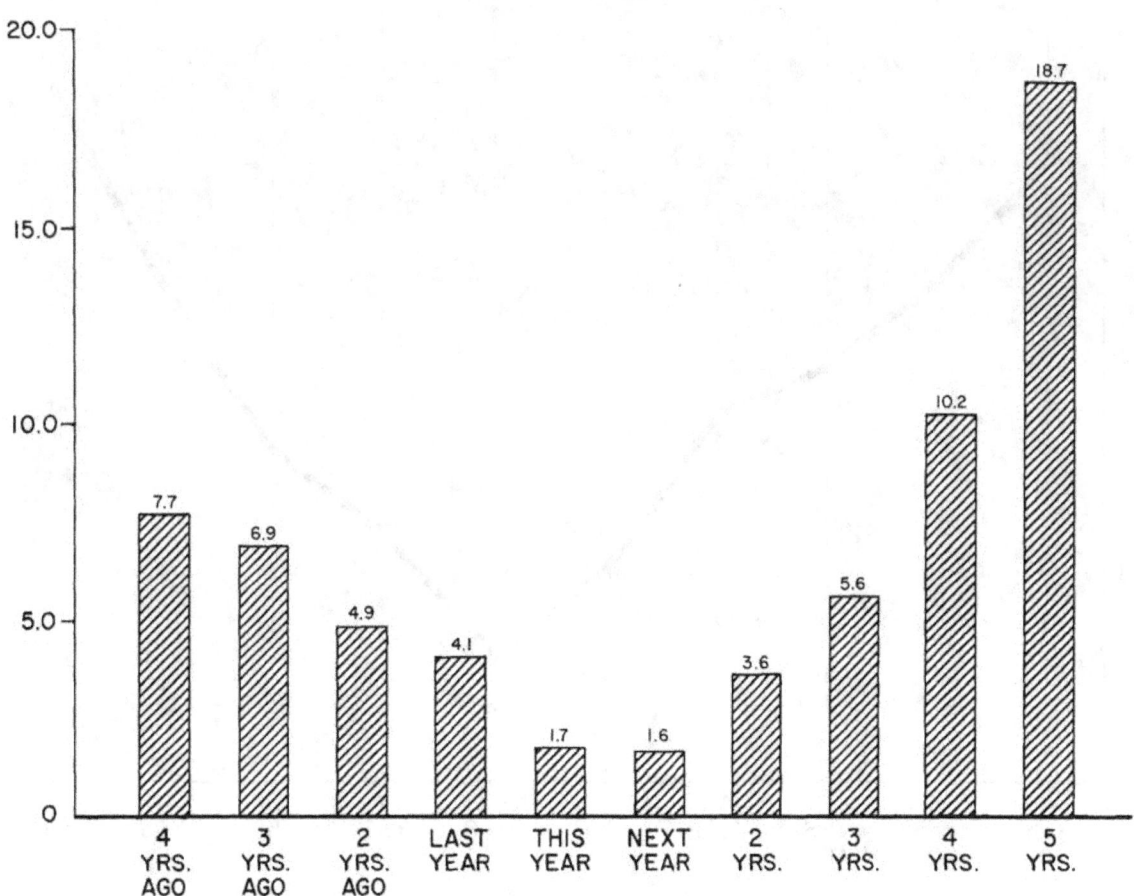

CHART 29

THE FRANCIS COMPANY
• MOTOR DIVISION •
PRETAX PROFIT % TO SALES

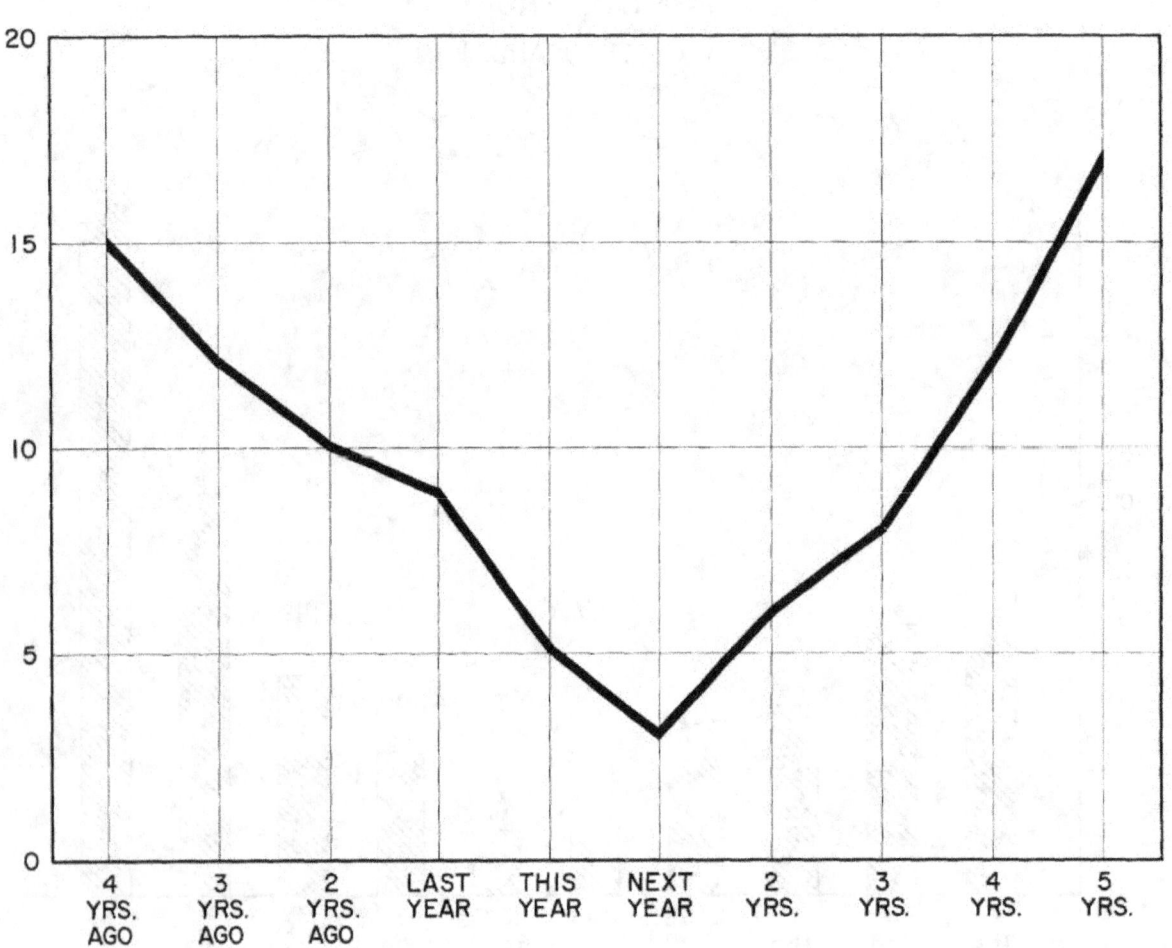

CHART 30

THE FRANCIS COMPANY
• MOTOR DIVISION •
% RETURN ON ASSETS

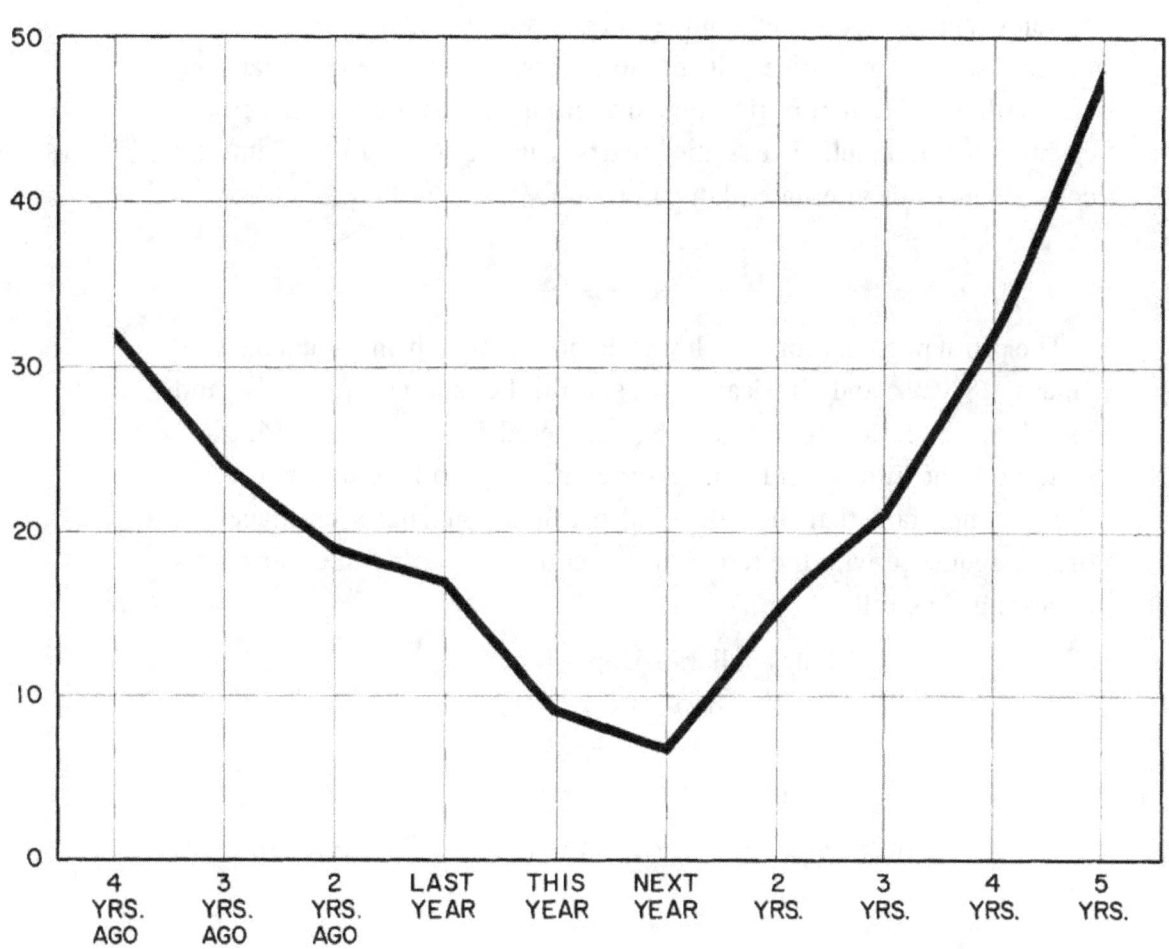

management must be made aware of the serious consequences of large cash outlays and expense buildups, if these are not accompanied by higher sales.

This type of profit forecast should require a detailed explanation of how the goal will be reached. These explanations should cover new product proposals, market potential, expected market share, pricing policies, anticipated costs, competitors, plans for additional factories, warehouses, district offices, distributors, promotions, foreign expansion, etc. Without this support, the company should not commit the necessary cash and personnel. The same charts can be used to present the consequences of alternate plans of action.

———————————

The profit presentation which was demonstrated on an annual basis in charts 28, 29, and 30, can and should be shown quarterly and monthly. The following four charts, numbered 31, 32, 33, and 34, illustrate how the annual and quarterly technique can be combined.

It is important that the sales and profit dollar charts be placed in proper sequence with the ratios. It is recommended that the four charts be arranged as follows:

> Sales dollars—Upper left
> Profit dollars—Lower left
> Return on Assets—Upper right
> Profit % to sales—Lower right

The following schedule provides the statistics for these four important charts.

CHARTS 31 THROUGH 34

EXHIBIT FOR CHARTS 31, 32, 33, and 34

THE FRANCIS COMPANY
MOTOR DIVISION

Sales, Pretax Profits, % to Sales
and % Return on Assets
Last Year, This Year and Next Year
By Quarters

	First	Second	Third	Fourth	Total Year	Data for Chart Last
Year						
Sales	$ 8 000	$ 8 500	$15 800	$13 700	$46 000	31
Pretax Profits	$ 100	$ 400	$ 2 000	$ 1 600	$ 4 100	32
% to Sales	1.3	4.7	12.7	11.7	9.0	34
% Return on Assets	2.5	8.9	24.1	22.2	17.0	33
This Year						
Sales	$ 7 800	$ 4 200	$ 8 900	$13 300	$34 200	31
Pretax Profits	$ 200	$ 150	$ 500	$ 850	$ 1 700	32
% to Sales	2.6	3.65.6	6.4		5.0	34
% Return on Assets	4.4	6.19.5	10.9		9.0	33
Next Year						
Sales	$10 000	$12 000	$18 000	$12 000	$52 000	31
Pretax Profits	$ 300	$ 500	$ 600	$ 200	$ 1 600	32
% to Sales	3.0	4.2	3.3	1.7	3.0	34
% Return on Assets	7.2	10.0	7.9	4.0	7.0	33

CHART 31

THE FRANCIS COMPANY
• MOTOR DIVISION •

SALES
($ THOUSANDS)

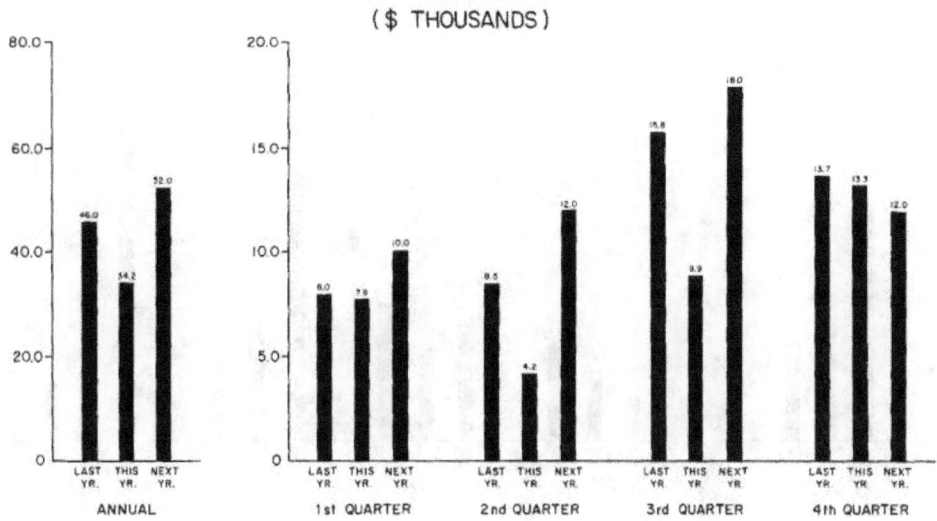

CHART 32

PRETAX PROFIT
($ THOUSANDS)

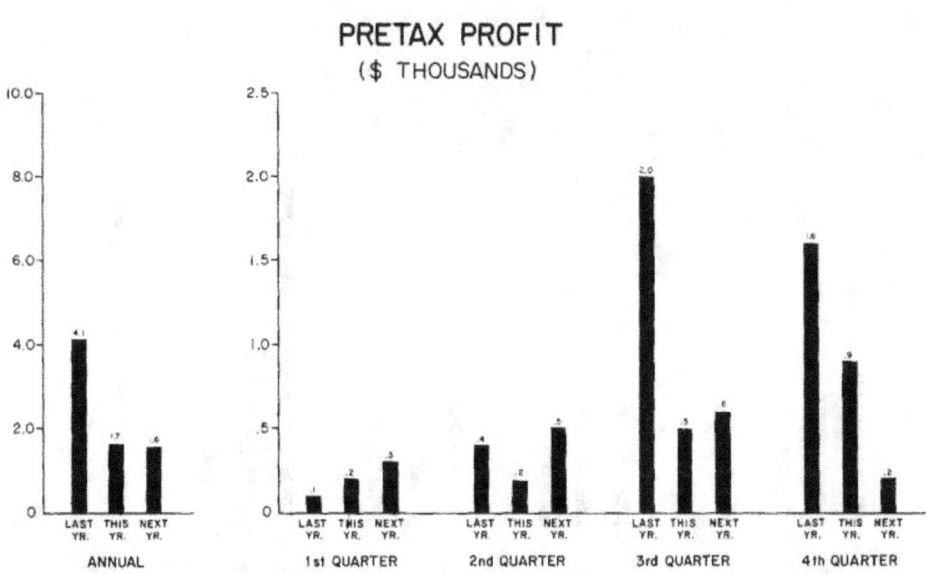

CHART 33

THE FRANCIS COMPANY
• MOTOR DIVISION •
% RETURN ON ASSETS

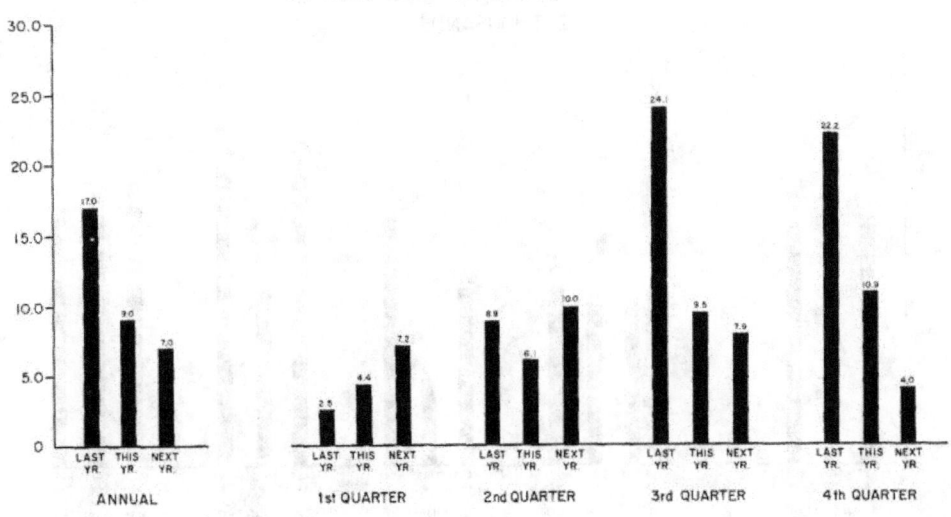

CHART 34

% PROFIT TO SALES

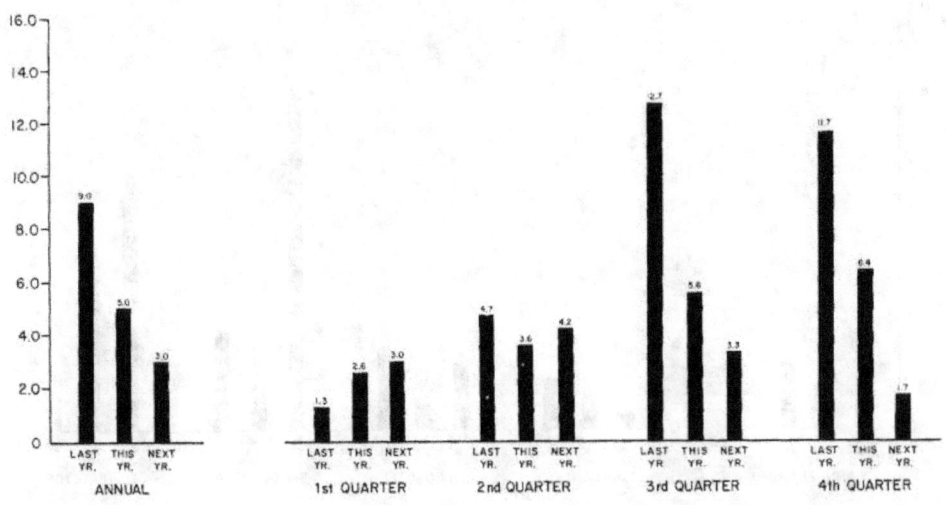

112

Comments

This is considered, by the author, to be one of the most effective of all types of chart presentations for management evaluation purposes.

If the four charts are so arranged that the sales and profit dollar charts are facing the ratios which they generate, the operating executive has a capsule view of the "action" parts of the business.

It is particularly significant, in this illustration, to note how the third and fourth quarter profit percent to sales and percent return on assets for next year are estimated below last year and this year, even though sales are much higher in the third quarter and only slightly lower in the fourth quarter. The charts show this at a glance, and require less study than is demanded by the statistics.

———————————

In order that the concept of bringing the sales, profits and ratios to the attention of management is clearly understood, another format is demonstrated.

In this illustration, annual performance is plotted on a line chart. This is inserted at this point in the book for added emphasis, and to enable those embarking on a chart program, full opportunity to form a judgment of preferred treatment. It is felt that if no other set of charts are used, these can be of great value to all levels of management.

These can be used to review total company, divisional or individual product line performances for any period, and for comparing actual versus budget.

The following schedule provides the statistical data for charts 35 through 38 which show annual performance plotted on line charts.

THE FRANCIS COMPANY
MOTOR DIVISION

Sales, Pretax Profits, % to Sales and
% Return on Assets Annually—Past 5
Years and Next 5 Years

	Profits	Pretax Sales	% to Assets	Average Assets	% Return on Sales
4 Years Ago	$ 51 500	$ 7 700	15	$20 000	39
3 Years Ago	57 200	6 900	12	30 000	23
2 Years Ago	49 200	4 900	10	27 000	18
Last Year	46 000	4 100	9	24 000	17
This Year	34 200	1 700	5	20 000	9
Next Year	52 000	1 600	3	22 000	7
2 Years	60 000	3 600	6	23 000	16
3 Years	70 000	5 600	8	26 000	22
4 Years	85 000	10 200	12	28 000	36
5 Years	110 000	18 700	17	42 000	45
Data for Charts	35	36	38		37

Comments

This series of charts points out that once an operation runs into serious difficulty it requires considerable time to recover. In this case, a satisfactory increase in sales volume is accompanied by an upward expense trend and heavy investment in assets. This depresses both the profit ratio to sales and the return on assets.

With this type of a forecast, management is alerted to the necessity of taking immediate action to correct the situation faster. This can take the form of providing a better engineered product, possible price increases, eliminating staff department buildups, working with smaller inventories, turning receivables faster and possibly leasing instead of building new facilities.

CHART 35

THE FRANCIS COMPANY
• MOTOR DIVISION •
SALES

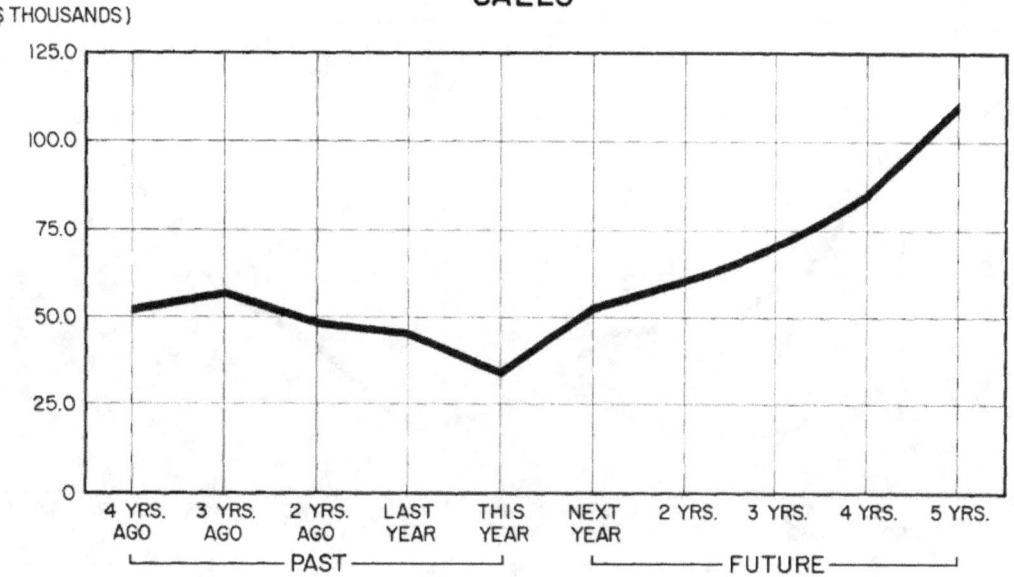

($ THOUSANDS)

CHART 36

PRETAX PROFIT

($ THOUSANDS)

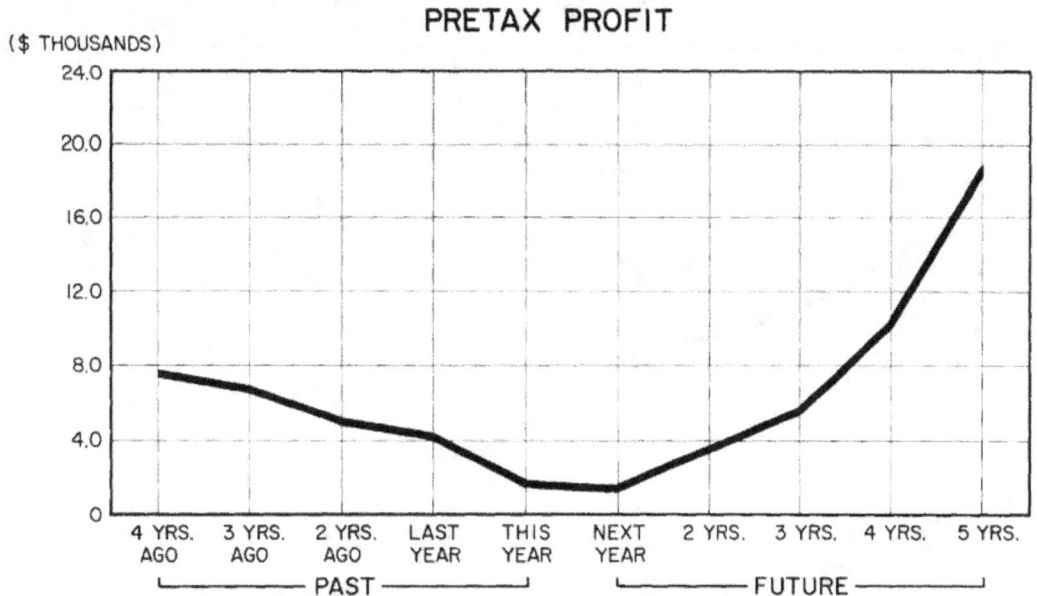

CHART 37

THE FRANCIS COMPANY
• MOTOR DIVISION •
% RETURN ON ASSETS

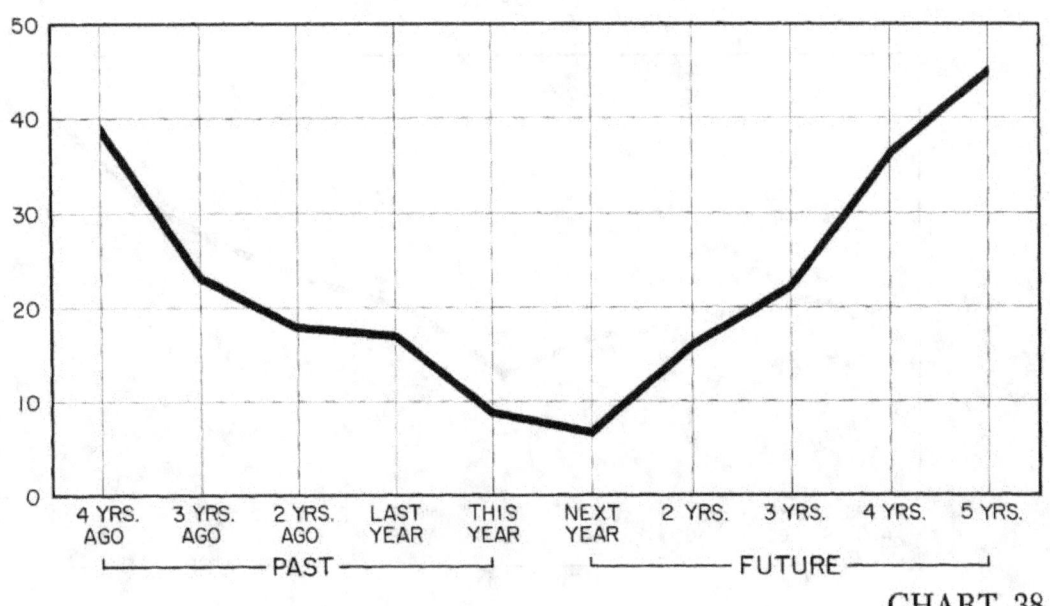

CHART 38

PRETAX PROFIT % TO SALES

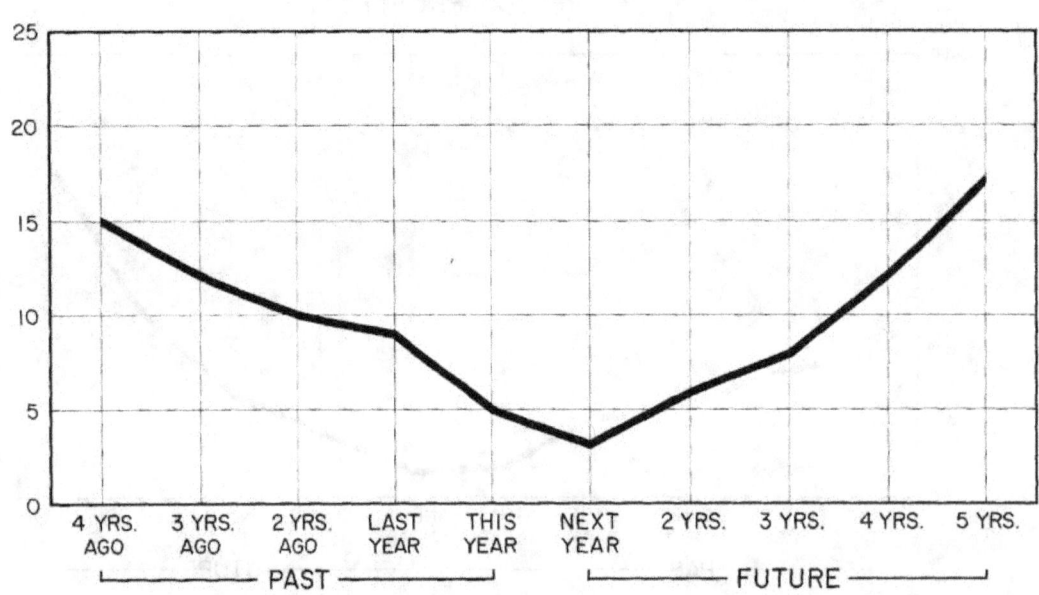

Competitor Comparisons

There are a number of important profit comparisons which can aid management. Several have already been demonstrated. However, it is sometimes not enough to compare internal results with budget, prior performance, or with other company operations. One very important series of charts compares a company, a division or a product line with its principal outside competitor. This is not always possible or easy; where possible, it should be attempted.

Care should be exercised in charting any aspect of a competitor's results. It is both fortunate and unusual if another company's total operations are directly comparable with yours. Where the other firm has a number of activities which differ from your product lines it is almost mandatory that an estimate of these non-comparable items be made. This is not easy and will not be completely satisfactory. However, it is better to provide an educated guess than to make comparisons which will be unacceptable to everyone and subject to continuing criticism.

The most practical approach to estimating a competitor's sales and profits by product lines is to contact your product line general management, sales manager, and merchandising and production supervisors. These specialists can usually analyze another company's business and supply useful guidelines. When it is necessary to fit a number of these pieces together, the job is somewhat complicated. It is possible, however, to arrive at general conclusions regarding the relative importance of a number of diverse activities. It is mostly a matter of patient research and common sense.

Chart 39 illustrates the shift of fortunes which has occurred in the Motor Division versus its number one competitor. This chart, illustrating the dollar profit and return on asset story, should be accompanied by a sales dollar and a profit percent to sales chart.

The following schedule shows the statistics for Chart 39.

THE FRANCIS COMPANY MOTOR
DIVISION VS. DIESEL COMPANY

Pretax Profits and Percent Return on Assets
By Years

	Pretax Profits		Assets		% Return on Assets	
	Motor Div.	Diesel Co.	Motor Div.	Diesel Co.	Motor Div.	Diesel Co.
4 Years Ago	$7 700	$ 6 000	$20 000	$28 600	39	21
3 Years Ago	6 900	6 500	30 000	31 300	23	21
2 Years Ago	4 900	8 500	27 000	33 300	18	26
Last Year	4 100	11 000	24 000	30 000	17	37
This Year	1 700	13 500	20 000	34 300	9	39
Data for Chart	39	39			39	39

Comments

It is helpful to a management to receive this type of comparison. This example illustrates how a competitor, which once lagged behind, has now outdistanced the Motor Division. This comparison will also help evaluate future Motor Division sales and profit projections which appear to be optimistic and which reflect taking a large share of the market away from an aggressive competitor who has proved himself.

CHART 39

THE FRANCIS COMPANY
• MOTOR DIVISION vs. DIESEL COMPANY •
% RETURN ON ASSETS AND PRETAX PROFIT

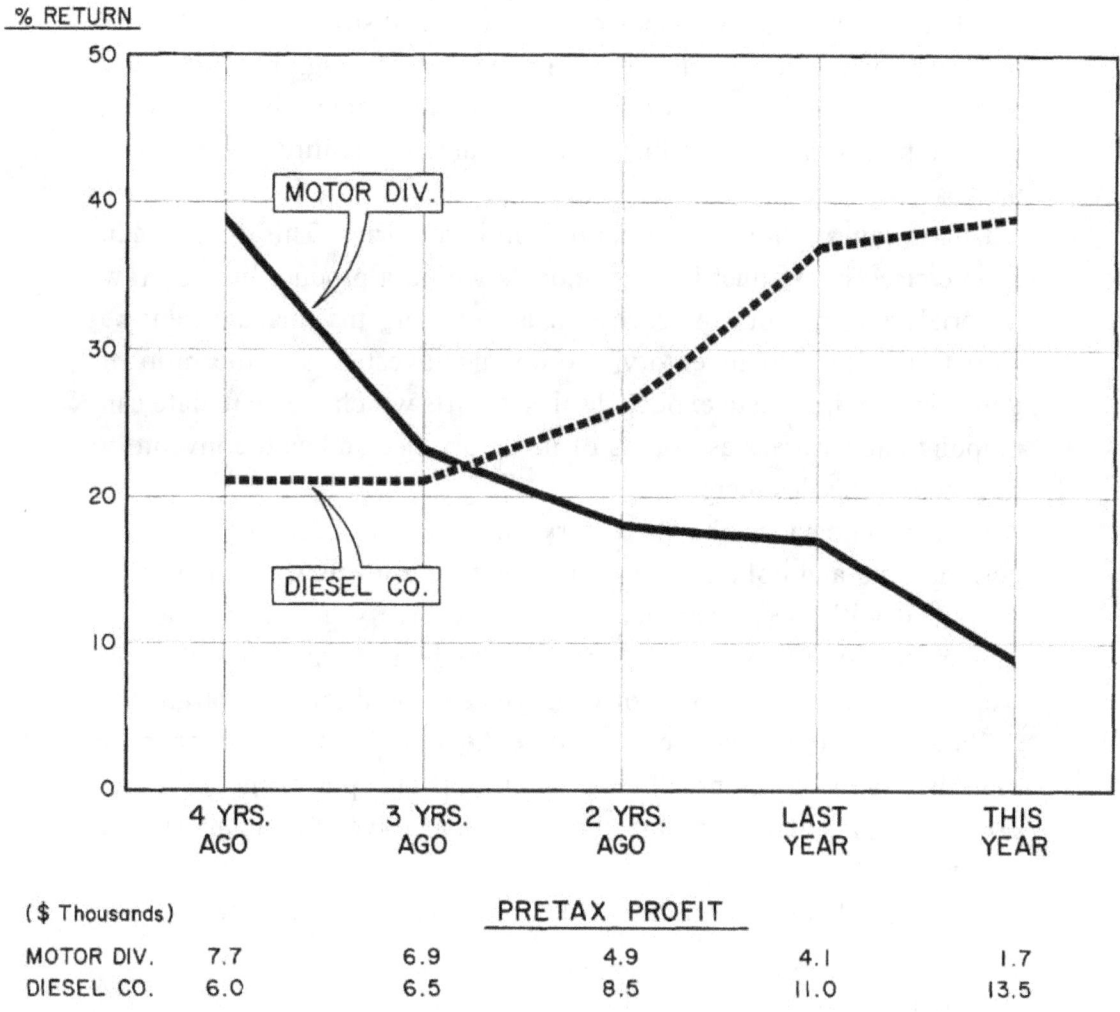

($ Thousands)			PRETAX PROFIT		
MOTOR DIV.	7.7	6.9	4.9	4.1	1.7
DIESEL CO.	6.0	6.5	8.5	11.0	13.5

10

CONTROLLING INVENTORIES

Operating profits are frequently reduced by the cost of writing off obsolete merchandise or disposing of goods at distress prices. An unbalanced inventory not only hurts immediate earnings but adversely affects future profits as a result of increased manufacturing variances, reduced prices, higher distribution costs, and an inability to move new models.

Charts can provide a tight control on inventories. This control can be exercised by product line, by models within a product line, by raw materials and by work in process. It is necessary that management be alert to the units of inventory, the dollars invested, and the ratio of goods in the pipeline to expected sales. Charts which are up to date can pinpoint danger areas as dollars of inventory rise and as the inventory ratio to future sales increases.

It is recommended that inventory charts by product line compare current units and dollars of inventory with the levels of the past five years and with the projections for the next five years. These can be further supported by other charts showing quarterly, monthly and weekly inventory positions for each year. In addition to plotting the dollars invested, the chart can indicate the number of days', weeks' or months' supply represented by the inventory. This places the units and dollars of inventory in the proper perspective for management evaluation.

It is possible that inventories have increased as a result of:

1. Changes in seasonal demand.
2. Increased sales potential.

3. Introduction of new or improved models.
4. Enlarged sales coverage.
5. New distribution outlets.

These and other factors could result in a satisfactory explanation of why inventory dollars are higher than in comparable prior periods. However, the weeks' supply should not also increase to any significant extent. It is important, therefore, that the inventory chart reflect *both* the dollars of inventory and the relationship to projected sales.

Charts should be used by management to show the probable effect on inventories if a new promotion succeeds as expected, has only mediocre acceptance, or fails completely. The chart then becomes an important tool for assessing alternate or corrective courses of action. In this manner dangerous inventory buildups can be avoided and profits can be materially improved.

The following charts illustrate these principles. A complete six months' program, by weeks, for sales, production and inventory has been prepared. The charts compare the annual rate of sales and production against the annual budget. The charts also compare weekly sales, production, and inventory position against planned performances.

This type of presentation can be applied to any period of time. The important point being demonstrated is that the relationship between sales, production and inventory buildup should be indicated, on both an estimated and an actual basis.

Annualized Sales Planning

The dollar comparison chart shows that while sales were declining, inventories were accumulating. This condition can only be corrected by expensive write-offs or liquidations at distress prices, unless the management acts to curtail production.

The following schedule provides the statistics for Chart 40 which indicates the extent to which annualized weekly sales are above or below the annual plan.

EXHIBIT FOR CHART 40

THE FRANCIS COMPANY
MOTOR DIVISION

Annual Sales Plan for Inventory Control
This Year By Weeks

Sales Plan $34,200

Week Ending	*Weekly Sales at Annual Rate*	Week Ending	*Weekly Sales at Annual Rate*
Jan.		April	
8	$38 300	1	$33 500
15	35 900	8	33 200
22	34 200	15	31 800
29	34 200	22	30 800
		29	29 800
Feb.		May	
5	37 600	6	30 100
12	38 300	13	29 800
19	38 000	20	28 000
26	39 000	27	27 000
Mar.		June	
4	37 600	3	25 000
11	39 300	10	24 000
18	38 600	17	23 500
25	34 200	24	21 000
Data for Chart	40		40

CHART 40

THE FRANCIS COMPANY
• MOTOR DIVISION •
ANNUAL RATE OF WEEKLY SALES vs. PLAN OF $34,200

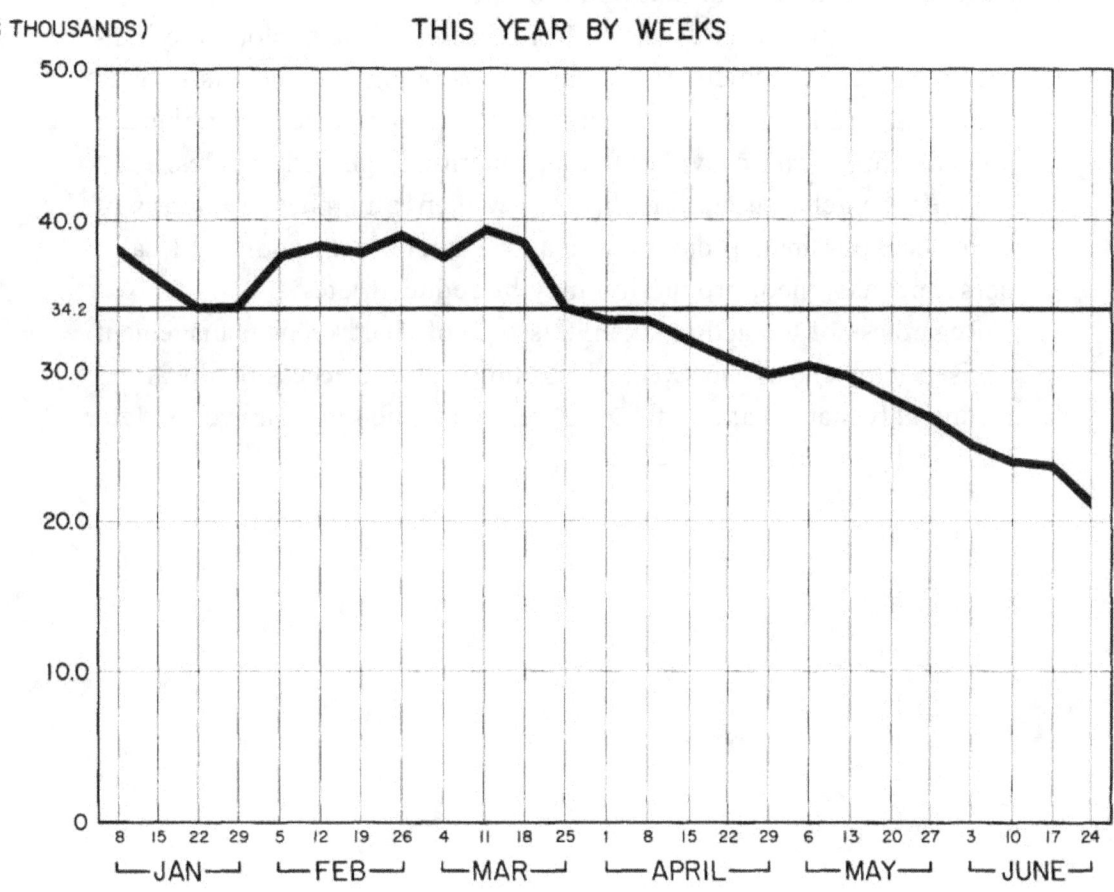

($ THOUSANDS)   THIS YEAR BY WEEKS

Comments on Chart 40

Annual Sales Plan

This chart indicates the planned annual sales level of $34,200 by a heavy horizontal line at that point on the scale.

The actual annual rate, derived from weekly sales, is plotted to indicate the extent to which the annual goal is being reached. As long as the actual trend line remains near or above the projected plan, there is no cause for alarm, provided that production is geared to sales.

When the actual trend line dips below plan, a number of courses of action are possible: promotions may be authorized, additional sales personnel assigned, production may be reduced, etc.

Regardless of the action taken, this type of chart keeps management advised at the end of each week. This eliminates the necessity of waiting for monthly statistical and financial reports, which may arrive too late for effective action.

Weekly Sales Plan

A second measure of sales vs. plan is to estimate weekly sales levels, on the basis of past performance or future expectations. Charts can thus indicate estimated sales fluctuations by weeks for a number of months ahead. It then becomes a simple matter to plot the extent to which weekly sales have exceeded or fallen below this plan.

The following schedule provides the data for chart 41, which illustrates the weekly sales charting technique.

EXHIBIT FOR CHART 41

THE FRANCIS COMPANY
MOTOR DIVISION

Weekly Sales For Inventory Control
This Year By Weeks

	Weekly Sales				Weekly Sales	
Week Ending	*Plan*	*Actual*		*Week Ending*	*Plan*	*Actual*
Jan.				April		
8	$657	$736	1		$ 600	$644
15	500	690	8		500	643
22	580	658	15		800	612
29	600	548	22		1 000	592
				29	1 500	573
Feb.				May		
5	900	723		6	1 100	579
12	700	736		13	1 000	573
19	500	730		20	875	538
26	500	750		27	700	519
Mar.				June		
4	500	723		3	900	480
11	500	756		10	900	461
18	400	742		17	1 300	452
25	300	658		24	1 500	404
Data for Chart	41	41			41	41

CHART 41

THE FRANCIS COMPANY
• MOTOR DIVISION •
ACTUAL vs. PLANNED WEEKLY SALES
THIS YEAR BY WEEKS

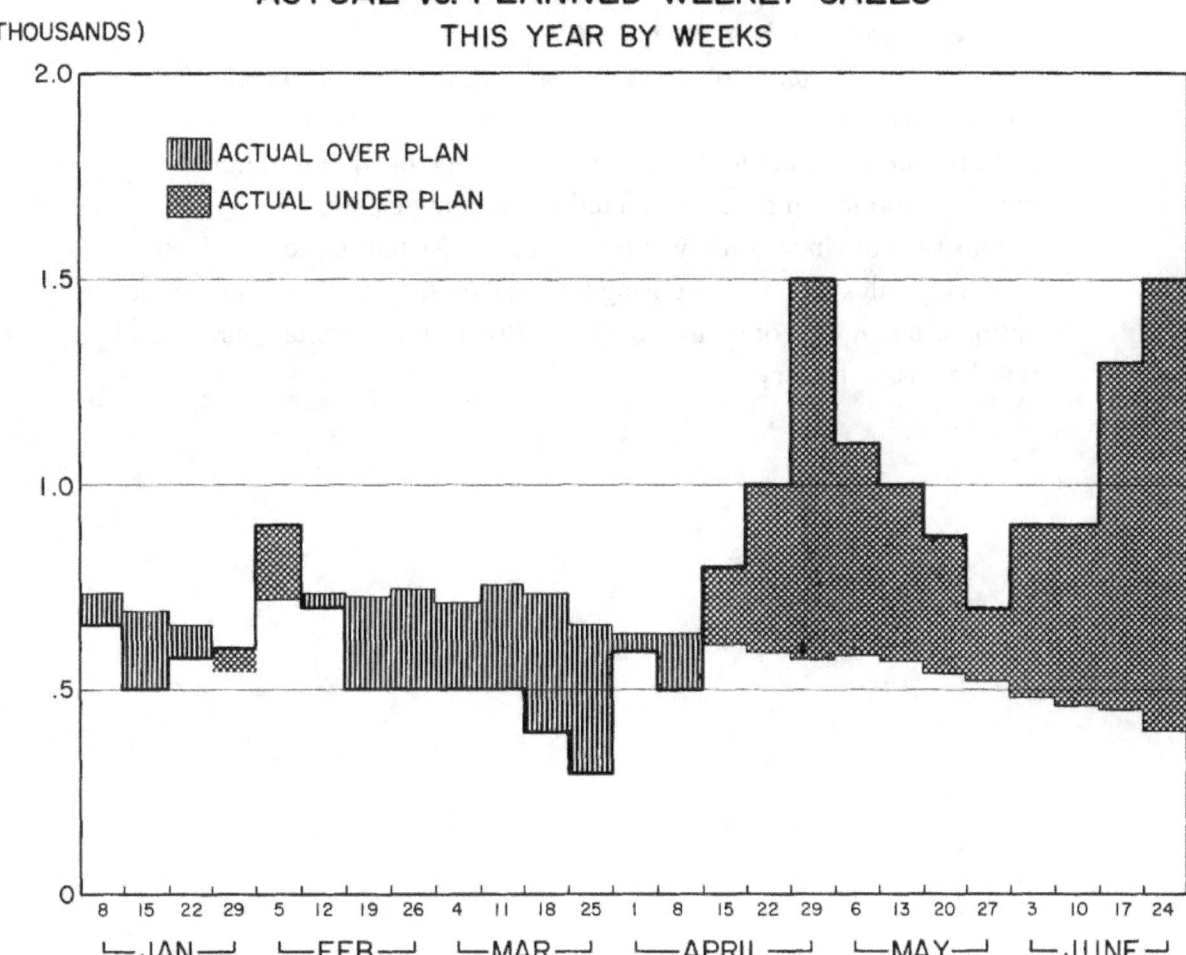

($ THOUSANDS)

ACTUAL OVER PLAN
ACTUAL UNDER PLAN

Comments on Chart 41

Weekly Sales vs. Plan

In addition to plotting the annual sales plan and annualized trends, it is advisable to have a chart which shows the extent to which weekly sales were above or below the weekly plan.

There are a number of ways of arriving at planned weekly sales: one is to average weekly sales for the past two to five years; another is to forecast sales fluctuations on the basis of planned promotions, new model introduction dates, expected price changes, etc.

This type of chart quickly indicates the consistent pattern and extent of weekly sales below plan during the first six months. Unless remedial action is taken, it is obvious from this illustration that total year results will be unsatisfactory.

Production Planning

Production planning is dependent upon the sales forecast. The production plan must consider level scheduling, labor availability and training, purchasing materials at favorable discounts, timing the arrival of raw materials, and warehousing the finished goods.

A weekly production chart, similar to the one on sales, is important in order to avoid an excess inventory if sales drop, or a shortage of product if sales exceed plan. The manner of preparing the production chart is the same as for the weekly sales series. It is demonstrated here to indicate the importance of its inclusion in the inventory control system.

The following schedule provides the weekly production budget and actual results shown on Chart 42.

EXHIBIT FOR CHART 42

THE FRANCIS COMPANY
MOTOR DIVISION

Weekly Production Plan For Inventory Control
This Year By Weeks

	Weekly Production			Weekly Production	
Week Ending	Plan	Actual	Week Ending	Plan	Actual
Jan.			April		
8	$800	$800	1	$ 500	$700
15	700	750	8	500	650
22	700	700	15	500	600
29	700	700	22	700	550
			29	800	525
Feb.			May		
5	800	750	6	900	525
12	800	750	13	1 000	525
19	700	750	20	1 000	500
26	700	800	27	900	500
Mar.			June		
4	700	850	3	900	450
11	600	800	10	900	400
18	600	775	17	1 000	350
25	500	750	24	1 100	350
Data for Chart 42	42			42	42

CHART 42

THE FRANCIS COMPANY
• MOTOR DIVISION •
ACTUAL vs. PLANNED PRODUCTION
THIS YEAR BY WEEKS

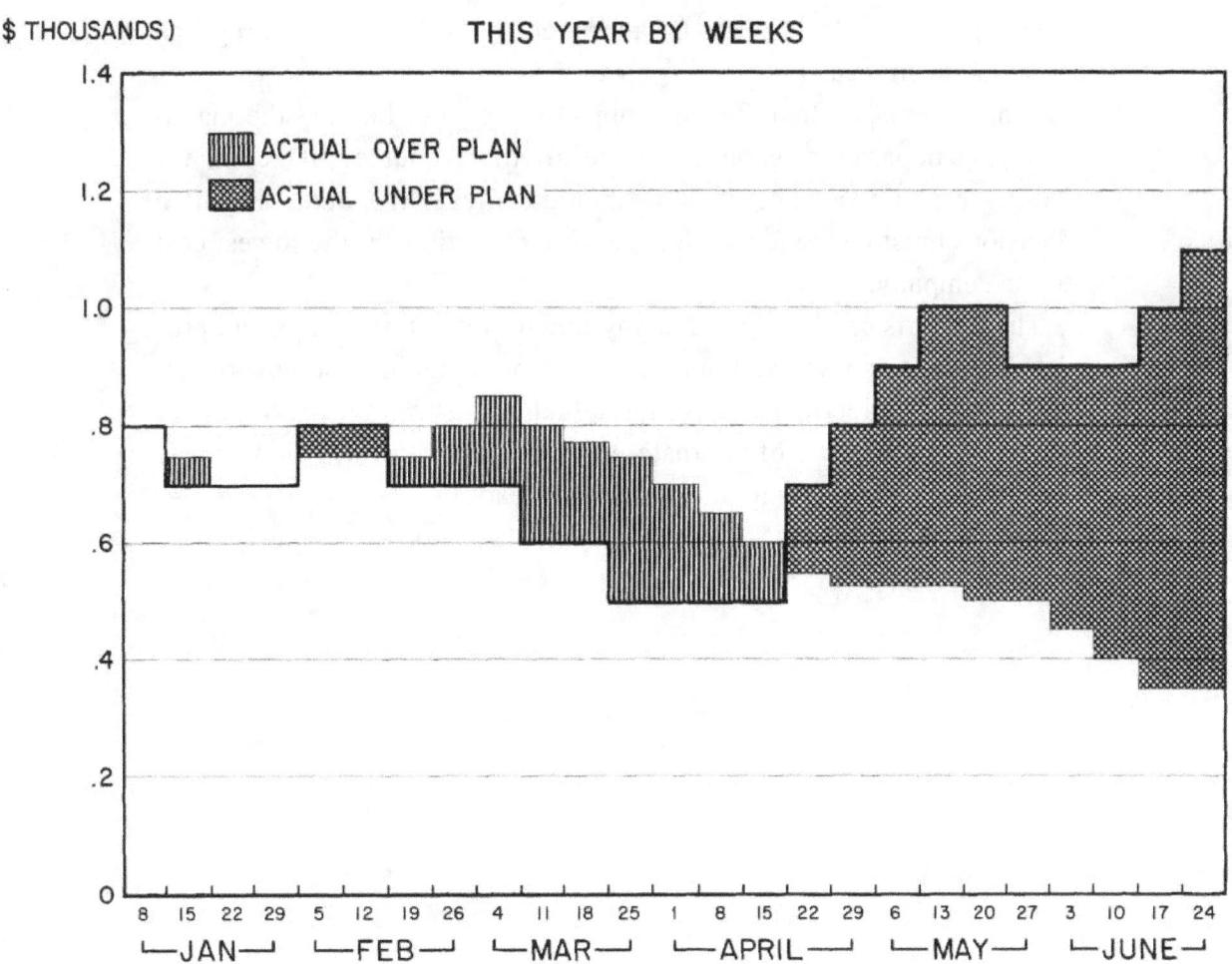

Comments on Chart 42

Weekly Production vs. Plan

This chart should be used in conjunction with the weekly sales chart. Level production should be planned, consistent with meeting sales objectives by models and the availability of warehouse facilities. This chart should be prepared after the sales plan has been adopted. The production plan should be approved by both the marketing and manufacturing heads.

When it appears that the sales objectives cannot be met, the manufacturing department should prepare alternate courses of action for cutting production. These plans should indicate the dates at which decisions must be made to effect varying reductions at the lowest cost to the company.

These charts can be revised at any time to reflect new sales and production plans and actual results can be plotted against the new objectives. It is not recommended that actual results be shown on charts which have a number of alternate plans; too much information on one chart becomes confusing and loses its impact.

Weeks' Supply of Inventory

The interplay of sales and production results in inventory increases or declines. These can best be expressed as days', weeks' or months' supply, based on projected sales. The management must decide, in preparing its budget, what it considers a normal inventory position. In the example used for the Motor Division, a seven weeks' supply was termed adequate.

Chart 43 shows how this critical inventory indicator can be kept up to date each week. The following schedule provides the statistical information necessary to plot the inventory changes which have taken place in the Motor Division over a six months' period, and how the situation compares with the planned seven weeks' supply.

THE FRANCIS COMPANY
MOTOR DIVISION

Weeks' Supply of Inventory This
Year By Weeks

Weeks' Supply of Inventory—Plan = 7 Weeks

Week Ending	Number of Weeks (Actual)	Week Ending	Number of Weeks (Actual)
Jan.		**April**	
8	18	1	24
15	18	8	23
22	18	15	22
29	19	22	22
		29	20
Feb.		**May**	
5	19	6	18
12	19	13	17
19	20	20	17
26	20	27	16
Mar.		**June**	
4	22	3	15
11	21	10	14
18	22	17	13
25	24	24	12
Data for Chart	43		43

CHART 43

THE FRANCIS COMPANY
• MOTOR DIVISION •

ACTUAL WEEKS SUPPLY OF INVENTORY vs. PLAN OF 7 WKS.
THIS YEAR BY WEEKS

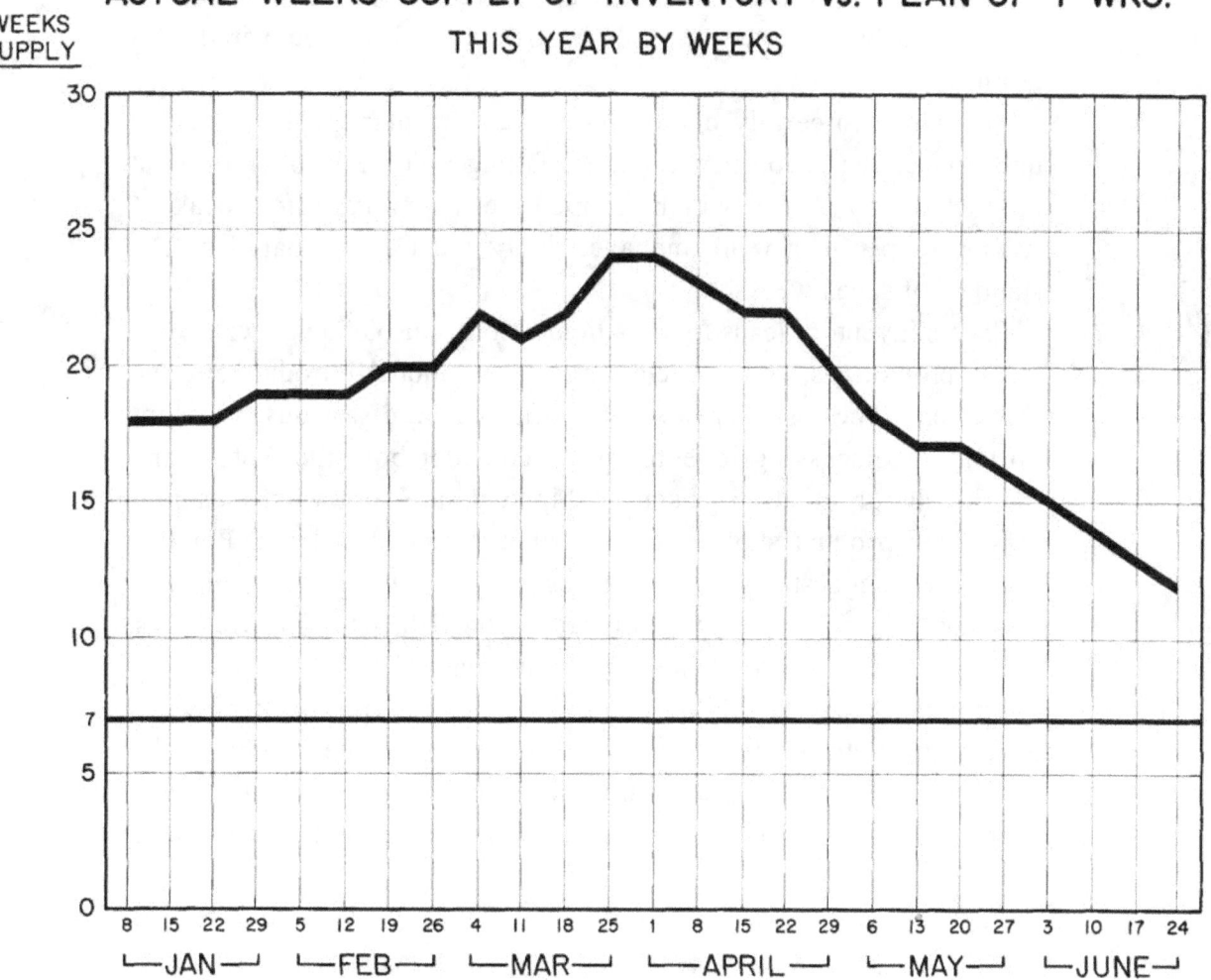

WEEKS
SUPPLY

135

Comments on Chart 43

Weeks' Supply of Inventory

This chart provides management with the most important statistic available on inventories; are they too high or too low; in balance or out of balance.

Dollars of inventory are important when assessing the amount of cash invested; but to the extent that an adequate weeks' supply is on hand it can be expected that this investment will be recovered, at a profit.

This chart forcefully demonstrates that the management decided upon corrective action in the face of falling volume. It obviously cut production to a degree which dropped the inventory from a peak 24 weeks' supply to a more manageable 12 weeks', compared with a standard of seven weeks'.

Excess inventory leads to sales liquidations, obsolescence write-offs, costly promotions, and the retarding of new model introductions and movement. The resulting loss of profit can be disastrous. It is important, in discussing inventories, to consider both the factory and the distributor situations. Factory shipments are somewhat meaningless if the product stays at the distributor or dealer level. For this reason, it is suggested that the weeks' supply be related to total pipeline inventory, which is the addition of factory and distributor finished goods.

This series of charts demonstrates the manner in which inventory control can be made available to management currently. It provides easy to understand information which ties together the important elements of sales, production and inventory for the purpose of improving profits. These charts become an essential tool for an alert management.

11

CONTROLLING RECEIVABLES

A liberal receivable policy may keep your customers in business, but it can be disastrous to your company's profits and cash on hand. It is necessary that management watch increases in receivables very carefully, both from the standpoint of dollar increases and from the ratio-to-sales angle. It is sometimes true that a more liberal receivable policy produces more sales, but this volume may come from the wrong customers. It also may be tying up more capital than the company can afford; or capital on which the company can make a better return in other areas. Charting the dollar trend in receivables and relating the amounts to sales can be highly profitable.

It is suggested that receivables be charted by division and by major product lines within the division, if this information is available and reasonably accurate. The chart should indicate receivable balances for each of the past five years, the current year, and the projection for the next five years. Quarterly and monthly charts should support the annual charts. All of these charts should show both dollars of receivable balances and the number of days', weeks' or months' sales represented by the receivable balances. Only one product line or division should appear on a chart where both dollars and ratios to sales are shown.

It is possible to compare several product lines or divisions on the same chart, if only dollars of receivables are shown or only the number of days', weeks' or months' sales ratios are indicated. *However, in order for management to understand and use the charts there must be a definite limitation on the quantity of information appearing on a single chart.*

The following schedule provides the statistical data used on Chart 44 to illustrate the receivable position of the Motor Division.

THE FRANCIS COMPANY
MOTOR DIVISION

Quarterly Receivables and Months' Sales
This Year and Last Year

| | Quarters | | | |
	First	Second	Third	Fourth
Last Year				
Net Receivables	4 300	6 500	15 800	9 100
Months' Sales	1.6	2.3	3.0	2.0
This Year				
Net Receivables	3 600	2 100	8 300	6 200
Months' Sales	1.4	1.5	2.8	1.4
Data for Chart	44	44	44	44

Comments

Receivables, like inventories, must be controlled. In the same manner, dollar sales increases in receivables must be evaluated in the light of months' sales. If the dollar total increases but the number of months' sales ratio declines, the management can be less concerned; investigation is required when the ratio starts up, even though the dollars may be trending downward.

This type of chart places both the dollars and the ratios for each quarter in the proper perspective. When the situation deteriorates the management should demand explanations; perhaps the entire credit and collection policy needs review. It may be discovered that special promotional terms are being applied to normal sales, that unwarranted discounts are being taken, that too many small customers comprise the largest percentage of overdue accounts.

This chart can be a valuable aid to management when the company has a substantial investment in receivables.

CHART 44

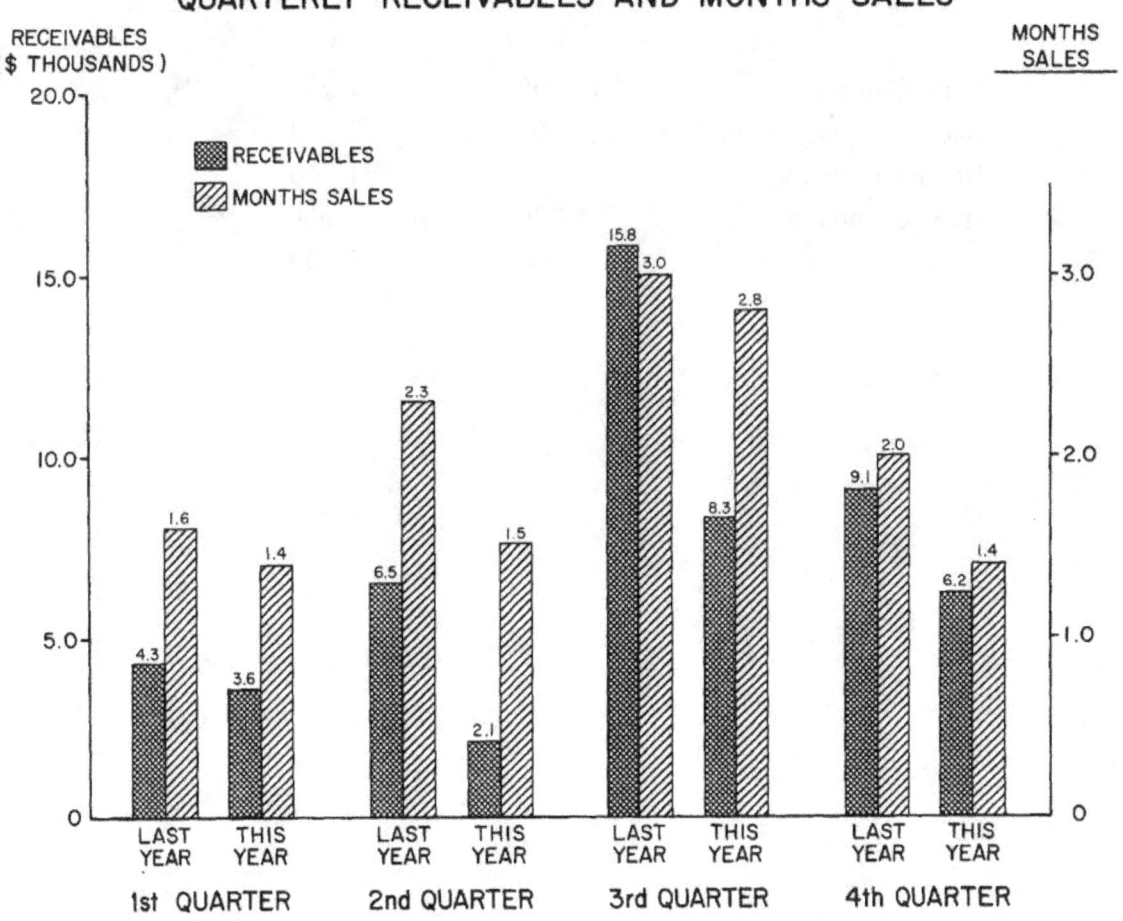

THE FRANCIS COMPANY
• MOTOR DIVISION •
QUARTERLY RECEIVABLES AND MONTHS SALES

RECEIVABLES
($ THOUSANDS)

MONTHS
SALES

RECEIVABLES
MONTHS SALES

1st QUARTER   2nd QUARTER   3rd QUARTER   4th QUARTER

EXHIBIT FOR CHART 45

THE FRANCIS COMPANY MOTOR
DIVISION

Customer Sales and Receivables
Last Year

	Sales	Receivables
	$	$
White Company	10 000	4 000
Black Company	15 000	2 500
Brown Company	8 000	1 000
Green Company	5 000	500
Others	8 000	1 100

CHART 45

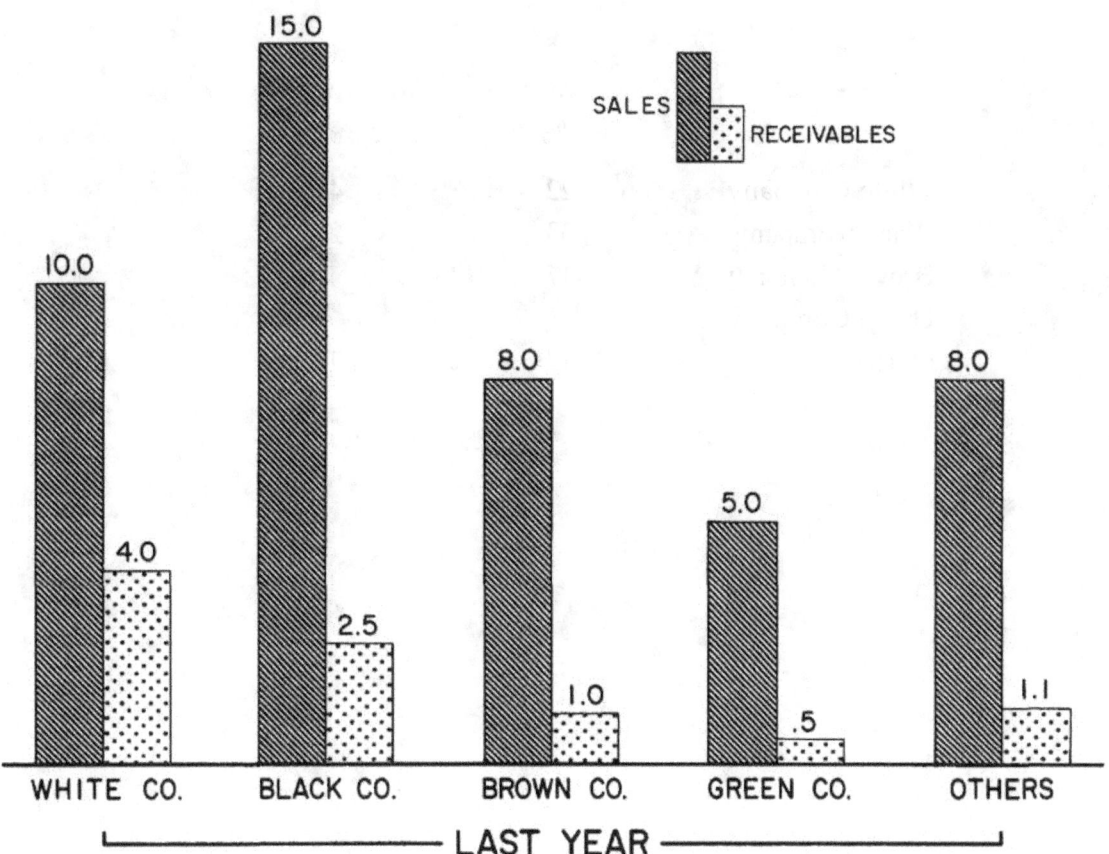

THE FRANCIS COMPANY
• MOTOR DIVISION •
CUSTOMER SALES & RECEIVABLES
($ THOUSANDS)

SALES
RECEIVABLES

15.0

10.0

8.0   8.0

5.0

4.0

2.5

1.0   .5   1.1

WHITE CO.   BLACK CO.   BROWN CO.   GREEN CO.   OTHERS

— LAST YEAR —

EXHIBIT FOR CHART 46

THE FRANCIS COMPANY
MOTOR DIVISION

Ratio of Customer Sales to Total Sales Ratio
of Customer Receivables to Total Receivables
Last Year

	Sales %	Receivables , %
White Company	22	44
Black Company	33	27
Brown Company	17	11
Green Company	11	5
Others	17	12

CHART 46

THE FRANCIS COMPANY
• MOTOR DIVISION •
RATIO OF CUSTOMER SALES TO TOTAL SALES
RATIO OF CUSTOMER RECEIVABLES TO TOTAL RECEIVABLES

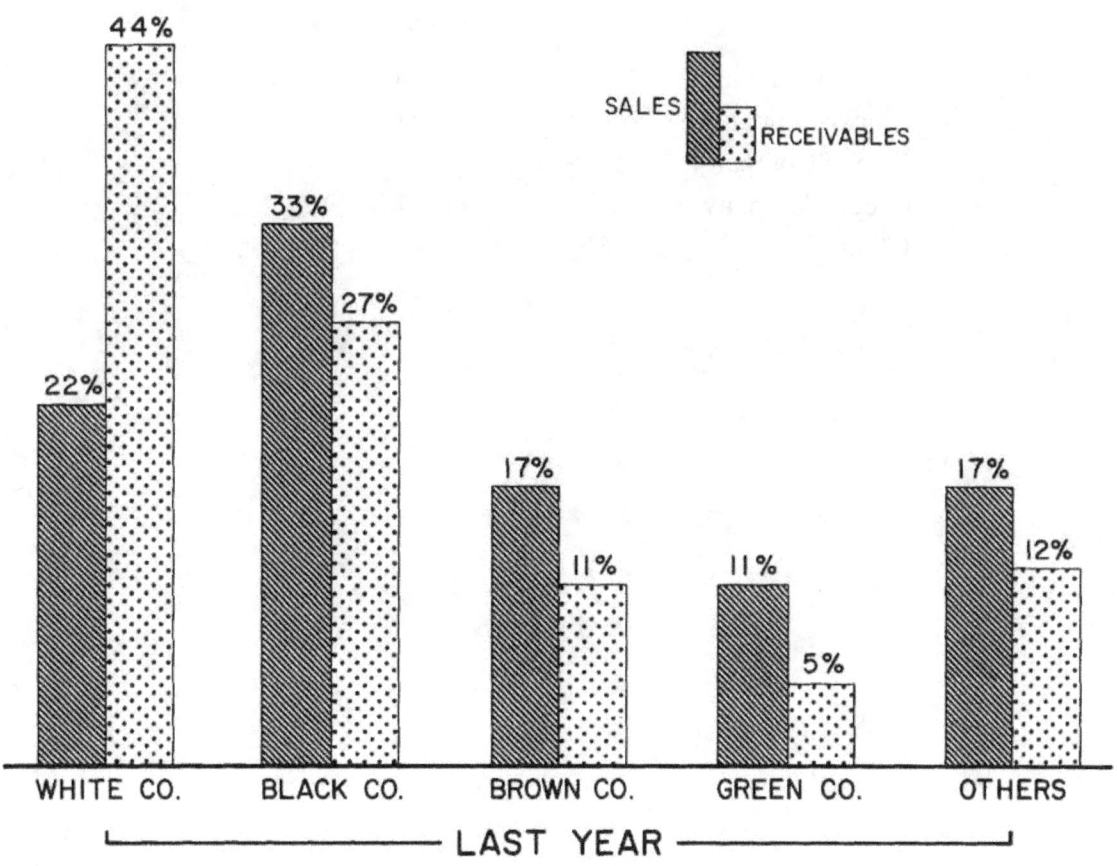

THE FRANCIS COMPANY
MOTOR DIVISION

Number of Months' Sales By Customer Last
Year

	Months' Sales
White Company	4.0
Black Company	1.7
Brown Company	1.3
Green Company	1.0
Others	1.4

CHART 47

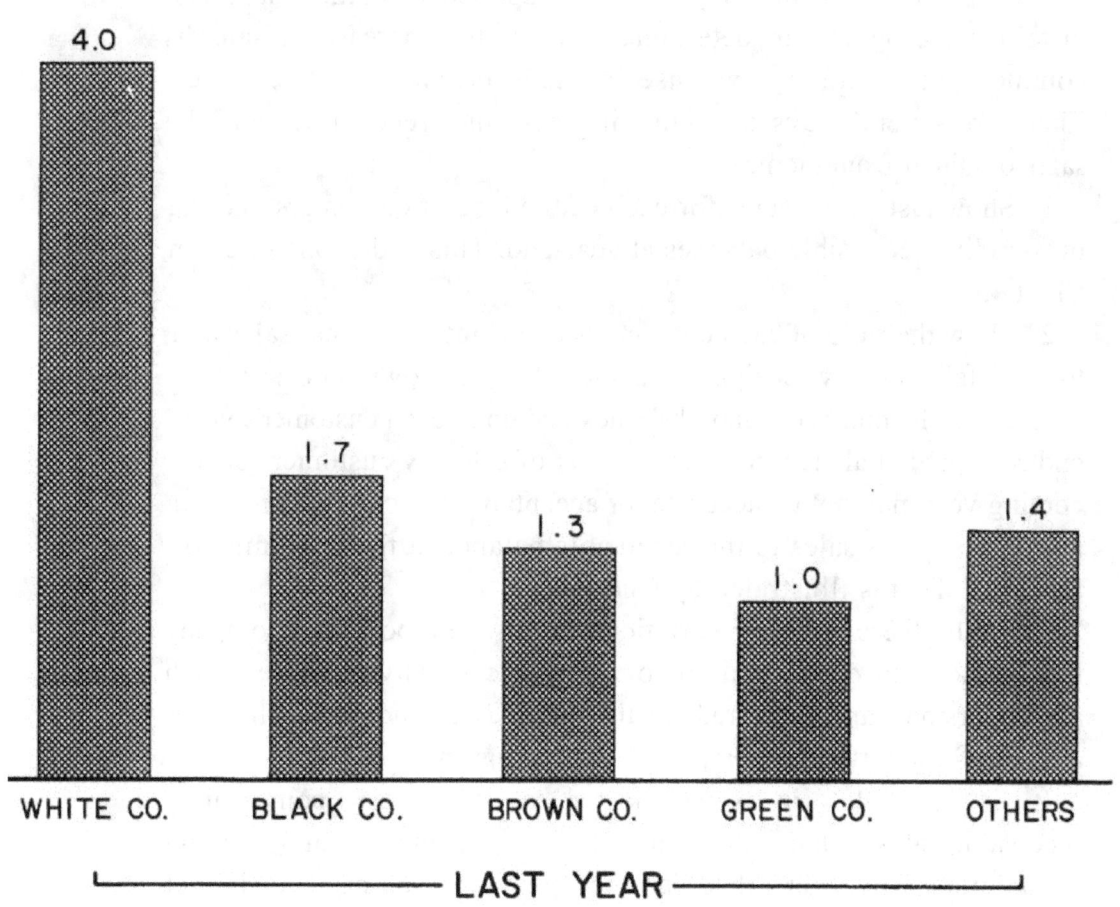

THE FRANCIS COMPANY
• MOTOR DIVISION •
NUMBER OF MONTHS' SALES BY CUSTOMERS

Charts can also be very worthwhile in comparing outstanding receivable balances by important customers and relating these balances to the volume of sales obtained from each. This can be most revealing and lead to corrective credit and collection policies which will free substantial sums for more profitable investment. It is often possible that customers have negotiated special terms during certain periods and then applied these terms to regular business volume. A trend chart will pinpoint the worst offenders and indicate whether a particular customer is receiving preferential treatment out of proportion to his purchases. This type of analysis can be applied to dating plans and installment programs to determine whether the increase in sales is commensurate with the increase in funds invested in receivables. There are several ways of comparing customer receivables and the sales obtained from them.

1. Show last year's sales for each of the largest customers and the outstanding receivable balances at year-end. This is demonstrated on Chart 45.

2. Show the ratio of each customer's contribution to total sales and to the total company receivable balance. This is shown on Chart 46.

3. Show the number of months' sales tied up in each customer's year-end receivable balance. Since a forecast of sales by customer for the coming year may not be accurate, or acceptable to your management, apply this year's sales to the receivable balance at the beginning of this year. This is illustrated by Chart 47.

Naturally there are other variations on how to report total company receivables and delinquent customer balances. Any of these which are understood and preferred by the chart users should be the ones adopted for a particular company's chart program.

It is possible, in some instances, to chart comparative receivable-sales relationships for the total company and leading competitors. However, this can be quite misleading and is not recommended when the companies involved are highly diversified or do not have similar receivable policies. It is recommended that, for best results, receivable charts concentrate on specific customers, individual product lines and divisions within the company. The proper charting of receivable information can be of great assistance to management if the area covered is not too broad and the comparisons do not become too general.

12

CHARTING THE ESSENTIAL
PROFIT RATIOS

Charts provide the most dramatic method for presenting the two ratios essential in running any business: the profit ratio to sales and the percent return on assets. It is necessary that dollars of profit continue to grow each year, but it is equally important that this profit increase at a rate commensurate with the rise in sales and assets. Charts very effectively plot this growth, or lack of it.

In order that a comprehensive understanding of the earnings relationship be available to all levels of management, it is suggested that the ratio charts contain profit percent to sales and percent return on assets for:

> The total company
> Each division Each
> product line

This information should be shown for:

> The last five years The
> current year The next
> five years

The near term comparisons should encompass last year, this year and next year:

> Monthly
> Quarterly
> Cumulatively

Wherever possible these comparisons should include the company's major competitors.

When these charts have been completed and become a part of the series which include sales, costs, profits, inventories and receivables, the management will have a clear view of its business. It will then be possible to display the four most basic charts, two to a panel, on two facing panels. These four charts, in the sequence in which they should appear, are:

Top left—Sales
Bottom left-Profits
Top right—Return on Assets
Bottom right—Profit Percent to Sales

This technique is demonstrated by charts 31 through 34 and 35 through 38 in Chapter 9; this type of presentation cannot be emphasized too strongly.

At this point, the people charged with the responsibility for operating the business have a capsule picture of where the company has been over the past five years, where it is now, and where it can be expected to go during the next half decade, based on current plans. If this 10-year story is unsatisfactory, changes in the plans can and should be made and then reflected on the charts.

The 10-year review can be brought into current focus by studying the monthly, quarterly and cumulative charts containing this same sales, profit and ratio information. The management is now in position to take corrective action. The story is plainly visible and the charts can quickly reflect alternate policies designed to improve profits.

These four charts summarize the sales and profit story outlined in the forward sections of this book. It is most important that these charts be presented to the management in a series of four, so that the dollar values can be seen in the perspective of the ratios they generate.

The following chart offers another approach, by combining the profit percent to sales chart and the percent return on asset chart. This technique is only useful when the annual rate of turnover is fairly constant; otherwise, the apparent trend line of the top bar, representing return on assets, becomes distorted.

This approach, of combining two ratios on one chart, may prove confusing to some managements, and is offered only in the interest of reducing the total number of charts required in a given presentation, or where chart space is restricted.

The following schedule provides the necessary statistics for this double ratio type illustration on Chart 48.

THE FRANCIS COMPANY
MOTOR DIVISION

Combined Profit Ratio to Sales and
% Return on Assets
10-Year Review

	Pretax Profit % to Sales	% Return on Assets
4 Years Ago	15	32
3 Years Ago	12	24
2 Years Ago	10	19
Last Year	9	17
This Year	5	9
Next Year	3	7
2 Years	6	15
3 Years	8	21
4 Years	12	32
5 Years	17	48
Data for Chart	48	48

Comments

This chart will indicate the extent to which profit margins have increased or declined during the past five years, and the degree of improvement expected during the next half-decade.

This type of chart also will show the effectiveness with which the management has utilized its total available assets. The extent to which the trend line for return on assets differs from the profit ratio indicates the degree of change in the rate of asset turnover. The ratios are developed by multiplying the profit percent to sales times the rate of asset turnover to arrive at the percent return on assets.

CHART 48

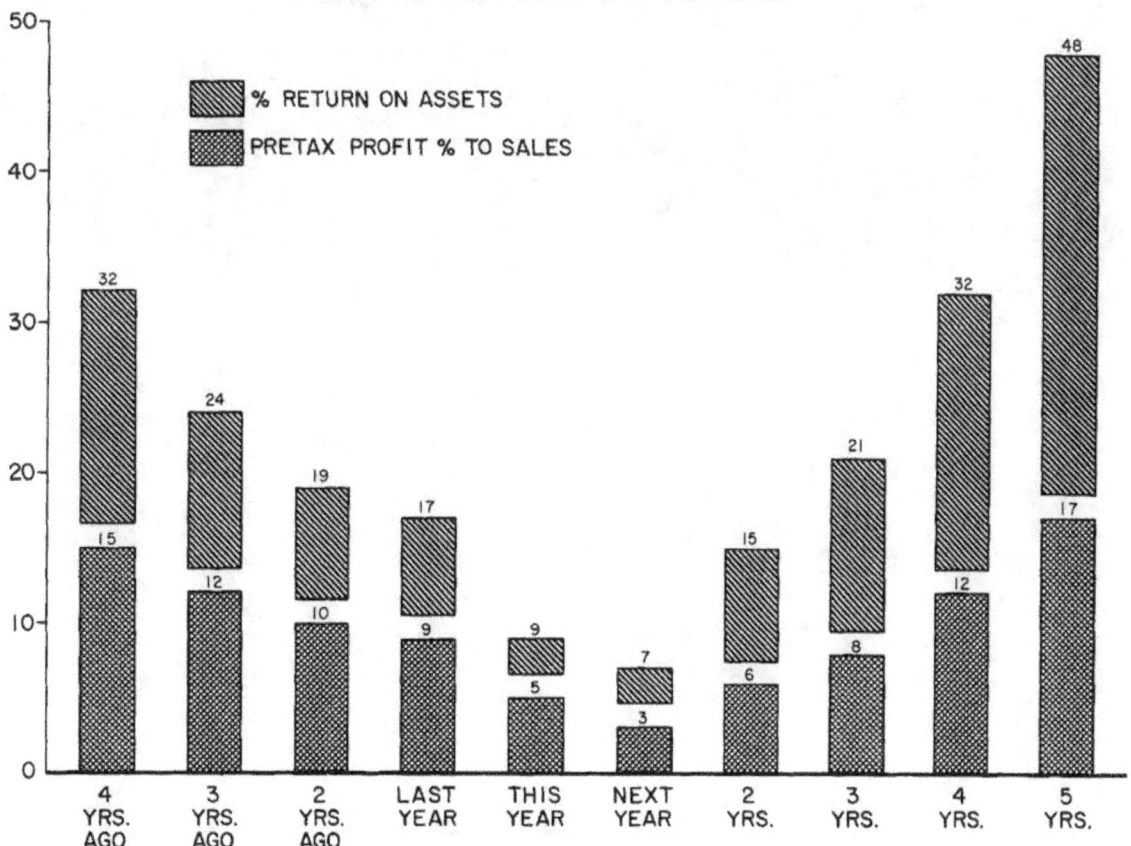

THE FRANCIS COMPANY
• MOTOR DIVISION •
COMBINED PRETAX PROFIT % TO SALES
AND % RETURN ON ASSETS

13

CHARTS CAN IMPROVE PROFITS

Conclusion

It is recommended that after completing this book the reader review several specific sections:

1. If the reader is the person who will *use* his organization's charts, he should devote particular attention to the sections on types of charts. For example, he should decide what kind of information will be charted first, such as sales, profits, return on assets, etc. At that time he should decide on the time periods to be used, annually, quarterly, monthly or weekly. When these determinations have been made, the chart user can examine the area of the book which illustrates how this information, in a particular time period, can best be portrayed. Not only are specific recommendations made throughout the book, but comparisons of alternate presentations are available. This allows each reader to judge for himself which method or style suits him best.

2. If the reader is the person charged with the *responsibility* for a chart program, he should become familiar with the necessary step-by-step procedures. This will permit a well-organized pro gram to develop with a minimum of confusion, cost, delay and disruption of normal reporting schedules. The chart program supervisor must also decide on what starting point to recom mend. He must also prepare several illustrative charts for execu-

tive review, along with sample explanatory material and a suggested format of the chart program. These should be prepared as a complete package and presented as a formal management recommendation. As a last step it is necessary to determine, in advance of any chart production, the source and timing of the basic data.

3. If the reader is the person responsible for *preparing* the charts, he should carefully examine the sections dealing with the necessary materials, chart construction, the use of colors and legends, the pitfalls to be avoided and the rules for good chart preparation. When the chartmaker becomes thoroughly familiar with the characteristics of a good chart, he will be in a position to guide the over-all program. This program is no better than the person preparing the charts, and he will contribute immeasurably to its success if he understands all its facets.

In summary, the author has attempted to make this book a constructive reference to the three groups of people associated with a chart program; the chart user, the chart program supervisor and the chartist. If properly conceived and fully utilized, *Charts Can Improve Profits*.

Also available from www.sunvillagepublications.com